D1343961

Sharing the Good News in C21

Evangelism in a Local Church Context

Stephen McQuoid

Stephen McQuoid is the Principal of Tilsley College, which is part of the ministry of Gospel Literature Outreach. He and his wife Debbie are also involved in a church planting work in Viewpark, Uddingston. Stephen travels widely, preaching in churches throughout Great Britain, and abroad, as well as lecturing in the college and writing.
His interests include football, scuba diving and reading.

Partnership

PARTNERSHIP GUIDES

Sharing the Good News in C21

Evangelism in a Local Church Context

Stephen McQuoid

Published for

by

paternoster
press

in association with Counties
and Gospel Literature Outreach

First published 2002 by Partnership and Paternoster Press

08 07 06 05 04 03 02   7 6 5 4 3 2 1

British Library Cataloguing in Publication Data
A catalogue record for this book is available from the British Library.

ISBN 0-900128-25-9

Cover design by Paulo Baigent.
Typeset by Profile, Culmdale, Rewe, Exeter.
Produced by Jeremy Mudditt Publishing Services, Carlisle,
and published by Partnership and Paternoster Press,
PO Box 300, Carlisle, Cumbria CA3 9AD.
Printed and bound in Great Britain
by Biddles of Guildford.

Contents

Preface

I sometimes feel a little uneasy in some of my lectures. It is not that I am unused to standing in front of people and expressing my views, it's just that when I am teaching a subject like, for example, evangelism, I am painfully aware that I struggle in this area just as much as anyone else. It makes me wonder if I have anything much to say on the subject. I am, of course, very committed to evangelism, as well as many other aspects of Christian ministry, but that commitment in itself certainly does not make me an expert.

As I began to pen this book on evangelism, I felt the same unease. I know many people who are better evangelists than I; probably they should have been writing this book. But whoever was to write, I felt that this was a book that needed to be written.

Evangelism has never been easy, but arguably it is getting more difficult all the time. In general, people in today's society are more sceptical about Christianity, and more entrenched in their worldviews, than any other generation in the past century or so. This world of unbelief has made the proclamation of the gospel a difficult challenge for Christians.

However great the challenge, and however reticent Christians feel about evangelism, this is an activity that we dare not opt out of. Jesus commanded us to take the gospel to the world. This was God's plan for church growth. In a very real sense, the survival of our churches depends on the extent to which we obey Christ's command in the Great Commission. But it is not enough merely to have the desire to evangelise; in a changing world we need to evangelise in a way that will be relevant to our society. It is for these two reasons that this book was written.

My prayer is, first, that as people read this book, they will be challenged to become more active in evangelism. Second, I pray that those who read will learn something that will help them relate the gospel more ably to their society. I write not as someone who has had enormous successes in evangelism, or as someone who claims to be some kind of authority on the subject. Rather I write as someone who has a passion for evangelism, and who has learned about the subject by carefully observing those who are experts.

There are a number of people that I would like to thank for the help they gave me in this project, either directly or indirectly. I should really begin with my wife Debbie who is very tolerant of her workaholic husband. It is not easy living with someone who always wants to get on to the next project. I would also like to thank my colleagues in the work of Gospel Literature Outreach. Their devotion to the cause of mission is a constant source of inspiration. It has been a privilege to serve alongside them, as a fellow member of the GLO family, over these past twelve years. My two fellow elders, Alan and Colin, are also an encouragement, and I have learned much from them, not least in the area of communicating the gospel. I must also thank John Allan who was an encourager and guide at the very beginning of this project. My grateful thanks to Dr. Harold Rowdon whose enthusiasm makes projects like this happen, and whose judicious eye picked out all the faults (hopefully) in my manuscript. Finally, thanks to Agnes who corrected those faults.

1

Help, What Do I Say?

I can remember well that awkward conversation. Although it took place on the main pedestrian thoroughfare that snakes its way through the heart of central Copenhagen, it could have taken place on any major high street throughout Europe. There I was with an enthusiastic group of young Christians witnessing to the people as they walked by that cloudy evening. We were on a summer team organised by Gospel Literature Outreach and wanted to use the freedom of expression so prized by Danes to bring the gospel to a spiritually needy people, so we held an open-air meeting in the most public place we could find.

Earlier in the week I had reminded the team that, although some of them had never been to Denmark and certainly had never shared their faith with a Danish person, yet they each had a faith that was relevant to all people everywhere and in every generation. Personally I was well aware of the significance of what we were doing. The renowned missionary thinker Herbert Kane stated that the gospel was universal because sin, the offer of salvation, the command to repent and the invitation to believe were all universal[1]. We were bringing to these people the only true message of hope that there was in a dying world and one which would never lose its relevance. The gospel is unchanging and does not need to change, because it is effective in every generation. The problem that day, however, was not going to be with the content of the gospel, but with my rather static presentation of it.

Our team was really quite good. They sang well and were able to perform some street theatre both of which were not only competent, but also enjoyable. Above all they were joyful and

---

1   Kane, *The Christian World Mission*, p.40

enthusiastic and many commented on how happy they looked. We ran several short, open-air meetings, and a significant number of passers by stopped to see and hear what was going on. As each presentation finished we moved into the crowd to engage people in conversation. It was at this point that I met my young friends.

Although with the passing of time I cannot remember their names, I vividly remember their faces and body language. This young couple were typical of many in Denmark and throughout Europe. They were in their mid-twenties and, having graduated from university, found themselves in the big world of work. Both of them were bright and were hoping to climb rapidly up the career ladder. They had a concern for the damage that capitalism was doing to the world and a compassion for the poor, yet at the same time they enjoyed all the benefits that their generous pay packets brought them and even took it for granted that they would live lives of comfort and prosperity.

This young couple were unmarried and indeed had little intention of ever getting married, but they were living together and were clearly committed to their relationship. They were members of the state church, but, like most Danes, that fact meant nothing to them. Indeed not only was their biblical knowledge virtually non-existent, they did not see Christianity as being any different from other world faiths. It was simply one of many religious options available to people in contemporary society. They had genuine doubts about the very existence of God and felt that if God did exist he must be very hard to find. It would be wrong to say, however, that they had no interest in the spiritual realm. On the contrary they held to several quasi-religious ideas that bordered on the superstitious. They believed that there were both good and evil spiritual forces operating in the world and that there was probably some form of existence beyond physical death.

I approached them for a conversation because, during one of our street theatre presentations, they were smiling and clearly enjoyed what they saw. For the sake of convenience I will call him Jacob and her Hilda, though with my poor memory I will never be sure if those really were their names. I asked if they had enjoyed the presentation and, when they said that they had, I asked if they understood what we were trying to communicate. Within a short time a good conversation had begun.

Coming from Northern Ireland I have never had a problem being direct with people. Within seconds I had launched into a description of the sinfulness of man and the fact that God is offended by our wayward behaviour. I then went on to talk about Jesus and his death on the cross which, I insisted, was the only solution to man's problem of sin. Next I explained how the work of the cross was able to remove all our sin, thus reconciling us with God, and I finished up stating how wonderful heaven was going to be and how much I was looking forward to getting there. Throughout this tirade I hardly drew breath and certainly never gave them an opportunity to respond to anything that I was saying. I felt happy that everything that I had said was theologically correct and was convinced that my sheer enthusiasm, or rather dogmatism, would persuade them to accept the truthfulness of my message. Unfortunately I was greatly mistaken.

Neither Jacob nor Hilda was put off by my veracious approach to evangelism, but they were not convinced by it either. Certainly they were amused to find a relatively young person being so passionate about something as old-fashioned and quaint as religion. But my whole approach, far from communicating the gospel, had served only to confuse them and drive them further away from finding God. To begin with, my description of the work of Christ and its effects was much too theologically advanced for them. I thought I was being simple and straightforward, but here was a couple who did not know what sin was and had no recognition of their spiritual needs. To them, sinners were murderers and child abusers. They certainly would not have seen their co-habitation as a sin and could not understand how a supposedly loving God would be so petty as to see their lives as being at fault.

What is more, they were not as yet convinced of the existence of a personal God. They knew about the theory of evolution and, although it did not entirely convince them, they were left in a position where they simply did not know what to believe. One theory seemed as good as another. Having been brought up in a thoroughly pluralist society, they were also of the opinion that every religion was equally true and valid and to disagree with this position was tantamount to bigotry. But there was another issue still. They were well off and lived in a country where the social services provided a network that would help them, were they to run into difficulties. In short, their lives were comfortable and this had led to a great spiritual complacency. Despite my urgency, they just could not bring themselves to seeing this issue as being of particular importance.

As we continued talking, the heavens opened and a heavy downpour began. It was an almost surreal experience carrying on the conversation in the pouring rain. As it was evening the shops had shut, so there was nowhere to take shelter. Jacob and Hilda did not seem too perturbed that they were getting soaked so I continued to witness to them. I shared my testimony and told them of the great joy I had being a Christian and having a personal relationship with the God of the universe. They were certainly interested in this and Jacob even declared, 'I am happy that you seem to have found answers to the questions of your life'. He was not being funny or sarcastic; I think he really meant it. But as the rain continued to pour down I knew that what was needed was not only more time to share the gospel with this couple who were genuinely open, but also a different approach. The gospel is unchanging but its presentation needs to dovetail with the understanding and cultural assumptions of those who hear.

Looking back on the incident I am faced with a number of more mature reflections. First, evangelism is not just about what we say but the work that the Holy Spirit does in the lives of those to whom we witness. We should never feel that the ultimate responsibility of reaching others is ours, or that we have 'blown it' if a conversation does not work out as we expected. The Holy Spirit is sovereign and we need the faith to believe that he can use our faltering words to convict people of their sin.

Second, although some people may struggle to understand the gospel when we explain it to them, it is nevertheless relevant and exactly what they need. Every time I share my faith with someone, I am forcefully reminded that this message is the only one that can change people's lives and the only hope of salvation. Any difficulties that I have had in sharing my faith have in no way discouraged me or left me feeling that I have nothing to offer people. On the contrary, with every difficult evangelistic experience I am more determined to try even harder next time, because I am ever more convinced of the truthfulness and necessity of the gospel.

Third, I am humbled as I think that God has entrusted the

majestic gospel message to ordinary people like me. It is one of the great wonders of Christianity that when God makes his appeal to the world he chooses to use ordinary men and women to do it. In this way although the ultimate responsibility of reaching others is not ours, yet we still have a responsibility to do all we can because God chooses to work through us.

Fourth, I am reminded that although the gospel message does not change and remains powerful in every generation, the way it is presented needs to change. We are not living in yesterday's world. We are living in today's world and soon it will be tomorrow. Our world changes and as it does, if we are to effectively reach the Jacobs and Hildas of this world, we need to think long and hard about how to do it. That is what the rest of this book is about and I trust that you will find it useful.

Questions

1 Think of a difficult conversation you have had when witnessing to someone who was not a Christian. What truths about the gospel did you struggle to get across to him/her and why?
2 What lessons have you learned from this and other encounters that you can apply to future evangelism experiences?

2

The Church in a World of Change

'*Go make disciples of all nations*' (Matt.29:19). With these words
Jesus gave his disciples the greatest challenge they would ever
face. Their task (and ours) was no less than to reach every nation
with the gospel, to declare to the world that salvation is freely
available as a result of the death and resurrection of Christ. Even
in those days with the world's population so much smaller than
it is today, the scale of the task was mind-boggling. In today's
world with its six billion people, its 7,148 languages, and its
complex geopolitical landscape, the task seems even more
daunting[1].

The greatness of the task is such that many Christians and
churches opt out of their responsibility, protesting that the job is
just too hard. Better not to get too involved and face disappointment, or so the argument goes. But the Great Commission
is for us also, and the luxury of opting out is not an option. Jesus
said: '*You are the salt of the earth . . . you are the light of the world*'
(Matt.5:13,14). It is not that we can be if we so desire; we are. The
only salt and light that our world will have is the church, and
that involves you and me.

But the job is further complicated by Jesus' command that we
should make disciples. It is not enough just to facilitate people
as they make their initial commitment to Christ. If that is the
extent of our ambition then we risk losing many spiritual babies
as they die of exposure in the hostile environment of our society. We are not to be mere spiritual scalp hunters. The task of
being a witness is not complete until the people we lead to
Christ have become spiritually mature and capable of maintain-
ing their own spiritual life. The whole focus of our evangelism

---

1   Johnstone, *Operation World*, p.1 (6th edn. 2001)

needs to change. We need to think long-term, not short-term. Our aim must be to bring people to 'full maturity in Christ' rather than just settling for an instant decision. Only then are we complying with the terms of the Great Commission.

Where can we start, for the world is such a big place? The only place to start is where we are. Every Christian should have a world vision and at the back of our minds should be an ever-present concern for lost men and women everywhere. But until God calls us to distant lands, we need to be active soul winners in our backyard. As individuals and churches the expression of our concern for the world begins by reaching and discipling people within our own community.

Culture

When the first disciples heard the Great Commission, they recognised that they needed to communicate the gospel within a set cultural context. The message of the kingdom required a form of communication which would relate to the people of their generation. This is the very essence of evangelism; making spiritual truths understandable to unspiritual people. To do this they needed to use the language of the devout Jew, the pious gentile, the Emperor-worshipper and those caught up in the Mystery Religions.

In much the same way we need to communicate the gospel within our own cultural context. Today's culture is not only chronologically far removed from the culture of the Bible, it is also far removed in its assumptions and thought processes. The world has undergone not one but many cultural revolutions since biblical times and we need therefore to grasp the essence of contemporary culture so that our presentation is as relevant to our contemporaries as the message of those first disciples was to theirs.

The need for making our presentation relevant and keeping up-to-date with current cultural trends will be an ongoing one. The rate of cultural change today is much more rapid than it was in the first century. Science, technology and the advent of the mass media have had an epochal impact on how Western society thinks and behaves. Whereas in past generations it took months and even years for fads to catch on, in today's world it takes days. During biblical times, if a citizen in Rome wanted to introduce a new product or idea to another city like Alexandria, it might take weeks for him to get there and share this new item with his target group. Today the Internet will convey an idea throughout the whole world in less than a second.

So where is society going? What world views dominate thinking in Western society? This is a big question and not one which I am able to answer satisfactorily. However, my experience of talking to people about the Christian faith suggests to me that there are a number of cultural presuppositions that do impinge on our presentation of the gospel. Many of these stem from a whole system of thought which is often referred to as postmodernism. This system of thought, though not universal, is nevertheless arguably the most influential and common of this present generation. It is important to look at what postmodernism is and then to see how it affects those to whom we are witnessing. Once we understand where they are coming from we can begin to communicate the gospel in a culturally relevant way. We must start by looking at modernity, against which postmodernity is a reaction.

The Advent of Modernity

Prior to the Renaissance, Europe as a whole was dominated by Christendom and consequently by the basic world view which Christendom espoused. Few doubted the existence of God or that human knowledge was ultimately derived from divine revelation. Most went to church and saw the institution of the church as the repository of truth. Many within Europe would have been aware of the existence of Judaism and Islam, but these would have been considered to be false religions and in some cases their adherents were even persecuted[2]. This stable cultural outlook was then shaken by the Renaissance.

At the heart of the Renaissance was Francis Bacon (1561-1626) who is arguably one of the first modern scientists[3]. Bacon emphasized the need for experimentation and believed that the use of the scientific method would lead to new discoveries as well as unify the sciences. He wrote about an ideal world in which science would become the key to a successful and happy society.

---

2   Groothuis, *Truth Decay*, p.33
3   Grenz, *A Primer on Postmodernism*, p.58

In the Enlightenment period which followed, theology was superseded by science as the arbiter of truth. It was the scientist who was at the cutting edge of cultural thought and not the priest. Whereas in the Middle Ages the church was the ultimate source of authority with God at its head, the Enlightenment ensured that human reason was crowned king. The leader in this revolution of thought was René Descartes (1596-1650). Descartes set out to devise a method of investigation that would discover truths that could be relied upon as certainties[4]. He did this by doubting everything but his own existence. He then affirmed his own existence by the reality of his thought processes. The rationale was that if a person was able to think, then the very fact that he was thinking was proof of his existence[5]. This theory was summed up in his famous expression 'I think therefore I am' (*Cognito ergo sum*). For him it did not matter what kind of thoughts he was having, the very fact that he could think was irrevocable proof that he did exist. This, he claimed, was the starting point in a search for certainty[6].

Descartes had a huge impact on subsequent thinking. Divine revelation was replaced by human reason as the starting point for knowledge. If someone wished to discover the truth about a particular subject, the surest way of making that discovery was to use rational thought and deductive reasoning. This new way of thinking led to massive changes in all disciplines of knowledge. This could most clearly be seen in the scientific work of Isaac Newton (1642-1727).

Newton attempted to show that the universe is an orderly machine that operates according to observable laws [7]. He was a Christian and hoped that once the universe was understood, those who studied it would be able to wonder at the greatness of God the creator. Certainly that was his own experience, but the scientific community merely saw their intellectual discoveries as evidence that science and human reason reigned supreme. The modern world with its irrepressible confidence in science and human reason had truly begun. Reason would now judge all areas in life from education to morality and theology.

---

4   Grenz, *A Primer on Postmodernism*, p.64
5   Brown, *Christianity & Western Thought*, p.180
6   Collinson, *Fifty Major Philosophers*, p.57
7   Collinson, *Fifty Major Philosophers*, p.67

From Modern to Postmodern

The pendulum, however, was about to swing in the opposite direction once more. Another significant cultural change was to take place. This change has become known as postmodernism[8]. It is not easy to state exactly when postmodernism began, but certainly a leading precursor was Friedrich Nietzsche (1844-1900), a brilliant philosopher from a pious Protestant family[9]. It would not be correct to describe Nietzsche merely as a post-modernist, for he really fits into the existentialist camp, but his ideas were remarkably similar to those of contemporary post-moderns.

Nietzsche declared that God is dead and suggested that once God is removed from the picture, human beings take his place and must recognise that they are responsible for the world. He taught that, without God, there is no basis for any objective values, meaning or significance in life, and this necessitates the abandonment of any concept of objective right or wrong. Nietzsche despised modernists who denied the existence of God yet retained Judeo-Christian values. It is not that Nietzsche rejected values or morals as such, indeed he realised their importance, but he insisted that we make our own values rather than discover them[10].

Nietzsche also abandoned the idea of objective truth insisting that truth was purely subjective. He stated that it did not matter whether a belief was 'true' as long as it was 'life-affirming', that is capable of giving those who believe in it feelings of freedom and power. Nietzsche's legacy was to produce a generation of thinkers who thought that human life was of little intrinsic value and that objective truth did not exist. This was not the start of postmodernity, but the intellectual conditions which would eventually herald the beginning of postmodernity were

---

8   Some scholars prefer not to recognise postmodernism as a separate cultural shift but rather see it as an extension of modernity, a kind of hyper-modernity. They do this because, although they recognise that the old rules of modernity have been passed over, there are many who nonetheless hold to many of the tenets of modernity, especially in the scientific world. Note Craig Gay's comments in *The Way of the Modern World*, pp.17, 18.

9   Russell, *History of Western Philosophy*, p.728

10 Reaper-Smith, *A Brief Guide to Ideas*, p.168

now in place.

It would be wrong to ignore the contribution that two world wars made to the general disillusionment with the modern world. The terrible inhumanity of Hitler and Stalin and that of later tyrants put paid to the idea that the modern world was making progress. While science was burgeoning, it was not making the world a better place or providing answers to the deepest question in life. Questions like 'Why do I exist?', the injustice of Western economies, and the negative impact that they make on the poorest countries in our world, put further nails into the coffin of modernity. The world was waking up to the fact that science and human reason were failing to deliver clean and uncomplicated progress[11].

According to most scholars, the cultural shift which took society into the postmodern era took place in the 1960s when many young people began questioning modern civilization with its social regimentation and technological advances. Some go as far as to state that postmodernism began on 15 July 1972 with the demolition of the Pruitt-Igoe housing development in St. Louis[12]. This trophy of modernist architecture which was built to be functional became so impersonal, crime ridden and depressing, that it had to be torn down. The modern world view with its rational basis and logical regimentation had become impossible to live with.

A Questioning of Truth

What then is the net effect of this world view change? Perhaps the most obvious contribution that postmodernity has made to contemporary culture is its questioning of absolute truth. In a world dominated by modernism, there was a general consensus that science could provide all the answers and make life better. Our postmodern generation does see the value of science, but recognises that science has also brought industrial pollution, gross inequality and nuclear weaponry. It has benefits, but flaws also. The result has been that postmodern man no longer sees science as the thing which will solve all man's problems.

But this questioning has not stopped at the door of the scien-

---

11   Cheesman, *Hyperchoice*, p.24
12   Veith, *Guide to Contemporary Culture*, p.39

tific world. There has been a more general questioning of sup-
posed truths to the point where few are committed to the idea
that absolute truths exist. This process has been greatly speeded
up by the advent of the global village and mass media. People in
the West are now continually bombarded with the cultures and
value systems of peoples all over the world. These have
inevitably been compared to Western culture and cultural values
and in many cases Western culture has been found wanting.
Increasingly we are developing an eclectic culture where any
value or idea can easily be assimilated. What was once considered to be true, correct and normative is now not seen in this
way. It is not so much that truth has been challenged, it is more
that there now is no truth in an absolute sense. Truth is merely a
matter of opinion.

Downgrading of Deity

Another result of this cultural change is that God has ceased to
be central in people's thinking. In one sense this is not a new
phenomenon. The Enlightenment and the modernist culture
which it spawned also questioned God. The theory of evolution,
developed by Charles Darwin, provided the sceptics with a nat-
uralistic explanation for the universe which removed any necessity for God. Science was then free to take the position vacated
by God.

The difference in the way God is viewed by the postmodern
world is that God is not opposed, he is merely downgraded to a
position of anonymity. In today's society you will find few people who argue aggressively that God does not exist. God has
been so devalued in most people's eyes that he is simply not
worth arguing over. It matters little, therefore, what view a person has about the existence of God, it will merely be interpreted
as his opinion and not some objective reality to which everyone
must acquiesce.

It is interesting to note that many people in the postmodern
world do not reject spirituality. Indeed, many would use tarot
cards and crystals and read their star signs in magazines and
daily newspapers. There is also evidence that people are drawn
to events to participate in a kind of mass spirituality. According
to John Drane this is exactly what happened at the funeral of
Princess Diana. He describes people coming onto the streets and

open spaces to mark their grief as a kind of pilgrimage, while others kept vigil by watching the proceedings on television[13]. But these forms of spirituality are not sustained by any concept of objective truth. Rather, they are the kind of subjective, experience-orientated spiritualities that fit neatly into the postmodern holdall.

Relativized Morality

The questioning of absolutes has also led to a moral framework that has been relativized to the point where it has become meaningless. No longer can a thing be considered to be right or wrong in a moral sense. Rather, the talk is of lifestyle choices. If someone chooses to engage in a homosexual relationship, or to experiment with recreational drugs, we cannot condemn him as immoral, for there is no moral yardstick by which his actions can be judged. Any objectors to his lifestyle choice will be dismissed as intolerant bigots. In this way the postmodern world has essentially abolished sin.

The media propagates this new moral freedom by handing the responsibility for this to the audience, who then decide how morals are constructed. Today's arbiters of morality are the talk show hosts who canvas public opinion and determine what is right. Oprah Winfrey and others like her will inevitably have much more impact on the nation's morals that any church or institution[14]. In the end, right and wrong will be determined not by any objective moral code, but by the personal taste of the individual. This will mean that morality will be reduced to its lowest common denominator. As long as you don't hurt anyone else, or mother nature, then anything goes.

Pluralism

What is true for morals is also true when it comes to religion. If there are no absolutes then no one faith can claim to be true in an absolute sense. At best a particular faith can be no more than true for the individual. Though the West is considered to be at least nominally Christian, the reality is that Christianity occu-

---

13   Drane, *Cultural Change and Biblical Faith*, p.80
14   Carson, *The Gagging of God*, p.24

pies no more space on the shelves of the spiritual supermarket than any other religion.

In a postmodern world all religions are equal, and equally true. They must all be taught in school and accepted as valid for those who are practitioners. The only heresy that exists is the suggestion that what someone else believes might actually be wrong. In such a world, evangelism is by its very nature abhorrent as it presupposes that what another person believes is in some way inadequate. The average man in the street is quite happy for a Christian to have beliefs, provided he doesn't expect others to become believers. Any attempt to convince someone of the rightness of Christianity will be met with questions about why Christianity is any different from any other faith.

In such a world the Bible carries no authority. Though it is the Word of God, it is not recognised as such. It is no more true than the Koran or Bhagavad Gita. At best it can only be pious religious opinion, but certainly not the unique revelation of God that Christians understand it to be.

Experience

A further effect of postmodernism is its obsession with experience. Facts have been replaced by feelings and truth by experience. I have already mentioned Nietzsche's belief that an idea did not need to be true as long as it was 'life-affirming'. That is, it gives the person a feeling of strength and freedom. The contemporary maxim, 'If it feels good do it', says more or less the same thing. Life is not built on objective truths but on experiences. Our actions should not be judged by any moral yardstick, but by whether we enjoy the experience of living.

It is important to understand that postmodernism is not just a philosophical idea that exists in the minds of an educated elite; rather its effects can be seen all around us. It can be seen in beautiful shopping centres where the experience of shopping is as important as obtaining the goods. Buying things for their usefulness is less important than the image and identity which the commodity can provide or the retail therapy itself. It can also be seen in the music industry where diversity and self-expression has produced a plethora of styles from reggae to rap and grunge to techno. We see the impact of postmodernism in the digital world where people clamour for the 150 TV channels which will give them choice, even though they will never have the time to view them all. It can also be seen in education where the teaching of historical facts is less important than interpreting the events, and in politics where image and sound-bite is a more potent vote winner than substance and policy.

It is into this society and cultural context that God has called us to be his witnesses and to make disciples. To a world where God is irrelevant and scripture carries no weight. To people who are confused with a mass of religious options all of which are considered to be equally valid. And to a society that does not believe in any sin except that of believing something to be absolutely true.

Questions

1 What examples can you see in your community of the impact of both pluralism and relativism?
2 How would you go about convincing someone that absolutes in morality and religious life really do exist?
3 What problems will we face in evangelism as we reach out to an experience-orientated generation?
4 How can the above problems be overcome?

Living in the Information Generation

In addition to the philosophical changes that have been shaping our society, there are other changes which have come about simply because we live in a world where nothing remains the same. In his epochal work *Future Shock*, Alvin Toffler likens the changes experienced in our society to a kind of 'culture shock'. He notes that when a person finds himself in a place where yes may mean no, where a 'fixed price' is negotiable, where to be kept waiting in an outer office is no cause for insult, where laughter may signify anger the result is 'bewilderment, frustration, and disorientation'[1].

Toffler's Future Shock

Toffler maintains that the future shock of the modern world is every bit as frightening as culture shock. The main difference is that, whereas a person experiencing culture shock can return to their native land and be surrounded by familiar things once more, the person suffering from future shock can have no such retreat. It is impossible to turn the clock back and prevent progress or change. It is not even possible to stay the same. Life hurtles on at a frightening pace and inevitably drags all of us with it.

When my grandmother was alive I frequently remember her complaining about the way life was constantly changing. I must confess that I got fed up with her criticisms of the society in which I was growing up. She seemed to be against everything from supermarkets to advertising. The way she talked gave the

---

1   Toffler, *Future Shock*, p.19

impression that the 'old days' were wonderful. The truth is that in many ways they were not. She grew up in a world where there were few rights protecting workers, where some of her contemporaries had to leave school at the age of twelve and find work, and where many people could afford only one pair of shoes. For her, however, the magic of the old days came not from any belief that life was intrinsically better seventy years ago, but because in those days she was surrounded by things that were familiar.

Now that I have a few grey hairs on my head I am beginning to understand a little of the fear that she experienced. As an evangelist I visit schools where pupils spend much of their time in computer labs and surfing the net. I left school before computer studies became part of the national curriculum and I find myself constantly trying to keep up with all that is happening in the world of information technology. When I was young I listened to Elvis, the Rolling Stones and the Undertones. The young people in my youth club have barely heard these names and they listen to music that I presume they find pleasurable but which for the life of me, I can't understand why. I remember enjoying geography, but now find a modern atlas confusing with all the name changes caused by disintegrating empires, young democracies and new sovereign states that want to return to their indigenous roots. Since beginning my working career I have also seen such huge changes in the workplace that I wonder if I will ever keep ahead of the game despite the benefits of ongoing professional development programmes. The truth is that future shock has begun to set in and I often struggle not to become as disorientated as my grandmother.

The Global Village

Not only does our world change, but the rate of change continually accelerates. Modern transport has shrunk the world down to a global village[2]. In 6,000 BC the fastest way to travel over long distances was by camel caravan averaging about 8 miles per hour. By 1600 BC the chariot was invented taking the speed up to 20 miles per hour. This continued to be the fastest form of transport for several thousand years. In 1825 the first steam

---

2   Toffler, *Future Shock*, p.33

locomotive came into service and it had a top speed of only 13 miles per hour. By the 1880's more advanced engineering had taken the steam locomotive to a speed of 100 miles per hour. This step had taken thousands of years. In less than sixty years, however, the speed at which man can travel had increased four-fold with aeroplanes in the early 1940's doing 400 miles per hour. By the 1960's rockets could do 4,800 miles per hour and men in space capsules could orbit the earth at 18,000 miles per hour. The far corners of the world are no longer remote. Indeed they can be accessed in a matter of a few hours and at relatively little cost.

If modern forms of transport have shrunk the world then television and the Internet have brought the world into our living rooms. We watch films that bring to life cultures from around the globe. As we turn on the news we are immediately informed about the terrors taking place in Afghanistan, landslides in Bolivia and the latest sporting events in China. There is even a National Geographic channel that ensures that no part of the world is cut off from the gaze of outsiders.

Linked with these multi-media developments is a huge increase in knowledge. Prior to AD1500 it is estimated that, in the whole of Europe, only about 1,000 book titles were being produced per year. This was due not only to the primitive methods of printing but also to the knowledge levels of the time[3]. By 1950 Europe was producing 120,000 titles per year. What previously would have taken a century was now being achieved in just a few months. By the mid 1960's this figure rose again to the point where, worldwide, books were being produced at the rate of 1,000 titles per day. Although today books are being produced faster than ever, the cutting edge of education is no longer the printed page but the Internet. A recent report in the Guardian suggested that in Britain alone Internet traffic was so huge that it equated to 360,000 e-mails per second and this rate was growing every month at the rate of 20,000 e-mails per second[4]. Scientists have also markedly increased in number, in particular over the past one hundred years. In 1910 there were about 8,000 British and German scientists and these made up a significant proportion of the world's total. By 1980 there were an estimated

---

3   Toffler, *Future Shock*, p.37
4   Julia Snoddy, *The Guardian*, 14 March 2001, p.26

five million research scientists across the world[5].

Although technology has undoubtedly made life much easier for many and lifted the burden of the mundane and routine from many working lives, it has not brought a liberation from pressure. Indeed the modern world economy has increased the pressure that we feel and has made stress a daily reality for everyone. Terms like 'industrial competitiveness', 'productivity' and 'unit cost' have become part of 'everydayspeak'. In every industry, companies are having to work harder to keep ahead of the game, and this in turn puts pressure on the workers who actually produce the goods. To go into business is to spend many long hours striving to keep up with the competition and fighting for increasingly small profit margins. While it is true that modern industrialised nations are providing their citizens with greater prosperity than ever before, it comes at the price of burnout, stress, broken marriages and neglected children.

In this materialistic rat race everyone must deliver productivity and value for money. Professions like nursing and teaching are not immune from this. Go to any high school or hospital and you will meet dozens of staff members who will tell you that their jobs are much more difficult and less fulfilling than they were twenty years ago. The pressure comes not just from the employer but from the high expectations that we as a society have cultivated over the last few decades. Everyone wants their detached house and expensive furniture. We all want to drive cars with central locking and heated seats. The luxuries which modern life has provided, like exotic foreign holidays, digital TV and designer clothing are now considered to be basic necessities. Without them life is just not worth living. The result is that we work harder and longer to purchase more, even though it does not make us any happier or healthier.

Human Machines

All of these changes can make society an extremely dehumanising place. A friend of mine who lives in London describes it as the most lonely place on earth. That hardly seems possible in a city of eight million people. He works in the 'city', a financial district where some 200,000 business people and office workers

5   Cheesman, *Hyperchoice*, p.24

ply their trade. Despite being surrounded by so many people, the area where he lives and works is nevertheless full of strangers who spend very little time talking to each other. Many of his contemporaries are so busy running around hectically being productive that they have little time for one another. What is true of parts of London is true of many big cities throughout Europe and the West. People do not make friends easily because our society does not value interpersonal relationships. We go to the supermarket and take our groceries to the checkout counter and never say hello to the cashier. They are human, and individuals in their own right, but society dictates that they are machines, just as the tills are machines. They are there to be productive not to be befriended. People are no longer people, but voices at the end of the line in a call centre or statistics in the job centre.

What effect do these changes have on the people to whom we are to witness? The answer is that they have a profound effect on how people view life. Our society is full of people whose lives are stressful and preoccupied with many worries and concerns. People also hear all kinds of voices and are subjected to information overload. In such a world it is difficult to know what is true and what should be believed. This has led many to ask the question, why should we believe anything at all? Our society is also full of people who are so taken up with materialism and the pursuit of happiness that spiritual thoughts barely come into their minds. They are too busy living for the present to prepare for the future. There are also many who cry out for recognition because they feel that they are nobodies.

All of these issues need to be taken into consideration as we go into our communities with the good news of the gospel. We need to be clear in our presentation so that we do not add to the confusion that people are already feeling. There also needs to be a recognition that people are at breaking point with so many pressures, and that our message must offer them the peace of Christ and a new set of values that will put our possessions in their proper perspective. We need to communicate the fact that we are each made in the image of God and are therefore unique and significant individuals whose every hair is numbered by a loving Father. Our churches need to offer the sense of community which society so lacks. If we recognise these issues then we have begun in earnest to fulfil the Great Commission.

Questions

1 What features of modern life make it difficult for people to commit themselves to the Christian faith?
2 What practical steps can a local church take to ensure that it remains relevant in a rapidly changing society?
3 What effect will the media have on the minds of the people that we are trying to win for Christ?

4

Where was the Church when Society Crumbled?

Having considered the changes that have shaped our society, we now need to look at the role which the church has played in all of this. The last one hundred years have been very exciting as far as the worldwide Christian church is concerned. In some parts of the world the rate of growth in the church has been staggering[1]. In Latin America and Africa in particular, God has been very evident in the lives of millions. The scene in Europe, however, has been somewhat different. Though the Roman Catholic Church is still a potent force across much of Europe, many Roman Catholics are increasingly nominal and apathetic[2]. Furthermore, the percentage of evangelicals in most European countries is very low.

If the figures throughout Europe give little cause for optimism, those in the United Kingdom are not much better. Statistics show that in the 1930's there were more than ten million church members, but today the figure has fallen to below six million[3]. The trend is still downward and affects most mainline denominations with the possible exception of the New and Pentecostal churches[4]. While it is true that many new churches are being formed, particularly because of the Charismatic movement, the mainline denominations like the Methodist, Anglican and Reformed, are shrinking at a more rapid rate than the new churches are growing[5]. This can be seen when comparing the demography of churches to that of society at large. In England,

1   Stoll, *Is Latin America Turning Protestant?* p.337
2   March, *Europe Reborn*, p.22
3   *Religious Trends* 2000/2001, No.2, 2.12
4   *Religious Trends* 2000/2001, No.2, 2.11
5   Sine, *Mustard Seed versus McWorld*, p.181

there are 25% more pensioners, and 30% fewer people in their twenties in the church than in society at large. The influence which the church exerts is also declining. One example of this can be seen in the fall of Sunday school attenders. In 1900 6,796,000 children attended Sunday school, which was about 55% of the child population. By the year 2000 this number had fallen to 530,000 or 4% of the child population[6]. Though Sunday schools are for the most part anachronistic and have been replaced by mid-week children's meetings, this rate of fall is dramatic and revealing.

The reality is that if you put all churchgoers of whatever persuasion together only 7.7% of the population of this country attend church on a regular basis and the number is still falling[7]. Even at Christmas time when church attendance climbs for the festive season, only 32% of the British population can be bothered to drag themselves out to a church[8].

These worrying statistics beg the question, why? What has caused the church in the United Kingdom to perform so badly, particularly over the past century? There was a time when it was the most natural thing for people to be christened, married and buried in church, but now the church has become a minority community in an ocean of ambivalence. Evangelicals in particular are viewed in a negative way. Clive Calver sums it up by observing that evangelicals are perceived to be a right-wing, fundamentalist, sectarian movement which is anti-intellectual, unconcerned about human suffering and imported from the United States[9]. Where did it all go wrong?

Slow to Wake Up

This question is a very difficult one to answer as it is so broad, but there are certainly some important reasons for the decline of the church and of Christianity in the United Kingdom. The first thing that needs to be observed is that the church has generally been slow to respond to the changes that have taken place in society. Culture moves on at an increasingly fast pace, but

6   *Religious Trends* 2000/2001, No.2, 2.15
7   *Religious Trends* 2000/2001, No.2, 2.14
8   *Religious Trends* 2000/2001, No.2, 5.6
9   Calver, *Britain on the Brink*, Ed. Martyn Eden, p.144

churches can often become calcified and tradition-bound, struggling to cope with the new world that confronts them. All too
often, Christians have been answering yesterday's questions
rather than tackling today's issues. Churches have been guilty
of holding onto structures that are well past their shelf life. In
short many churches have struggled to wake up to the 21st century.

The symptoms of this sleepiness are easy to spot. There is the
obsessive loyalty to old hymns. Of course many old hymns are
wonderful and timeless, but others do not relate to our generation and are sung to tunes that are a far cry from the contemporary music that people listen to today. In one sense, the songs we
sing in church are a small part of the overall package, but in
another sense when churches doggedly refuse to make use of
the many contemporary worship songs that today's writers are
penning, it shows that their whole attitude is one of unwilling-
ness to relate to contemporary society.

Then there is the type of services we hold. The Bible grants a
great deal of freedom to churches as far as their structures are
concerned. There is no one way of doing church. However,
some churches use the same structures and methods that they
did fifty years ago, even though people's lifestyles and attitudes
have changed markedly over that time span. The structure of a
church should be adapted to suit the needs of the people, rather
than expecting everyone to fit into the programmes.

There is also the way we do our evangelism. Sleepy churches
do not ask whether or not their evangelistic strategy is effective,
often because they do not actually have an evangelistic strategy.
Evangelism is just done the way it has always been done. The
only rationale behind this approach is that it worked in the past.
The point is that it was in the past that it worked, not now.

In all these areas the church has struggled to relate to a changing world and has suffered in the process.

Struggling with Liberalism

A second major reason for the decline of the church in recent
decades has been the struggle with liberalism. The rise of biblical criticism within the theological faculties of our universities
has made its impact on the church. Many of the assumptions
that had long been accepted in the church were beginning to be

questioned. Among the issues that began to divide churches was that of the doctrine of scripture.

Evangelicals have long held to a belief in the inspiration and inerrancy of scripture. In academic circles, however, the Bible was being cross-examined, both in relation to its textual basis and the extent to which mistakes appeared to be present. Methods of higher and lower criticism were being imported from Germany and causing many scholars to doubt, among other things, whether Moses wrote the Pentateuch[10].

It was inevitable that such issues would percolate down to grass-roots level. Though many evangelical scholars began to engage with critical scholarship, it was too little too late. A popular perception arose within society in general that the Bible was unreliable and could not be trusted to communicate God's truth without error. Many people who had never read the Bible for themselves would nevertheless have argued that the copying of texts from generation to generation meant that inconsistencies were common. The Bible was no longer held in reverential awe. To many it was a flawed book, and the debates on inerrancy that went on in the universities and between church leaders only fostered this view. With confidence in the Bible eroding, the church found it increasingly difficult to tell people that there was a message from God that they had to listen to.

Denominationalism

Yet another reason for the decline in the church has been the problem of denominational division. We now live in a world where different denominations appear to be sprouting up everywhere. Recent statistics suggest a total of over 30,000 denominations, and even in Britain the number is over 350[11]. This has done little to promote the idea of the body of Christ and many unchurched people have become confused with the vast array of different churches which apparently offer a slightly different slant on the same thing.

In a very real sense the evangelical church has been its own worst enemy. Jesus prayed in John 17:20–23 that all believers might be one. The model that he used for unity between Christians was his own relationship with the Father. He commented

---

10 Bebbington, *Evangelicalism in Modern Britain*, p.184
11 *Operation World*, pp.2, 650

that the world would be able to know that he had come from the
Father because of the unity in the church. Not only have Christians been divided, but their differences have all too often been
broadcast to anyone willing to listen. This denominationalism
has caused a great deal of damage and driven many away from
churches.

Holy Island

Adding to this list of problems is the fact that the church has
become isolated from the community. There was a time when
everyone got married in church and wished to be buried from
there. The church was the guardian of the nation's morality, and
when church leaders spoke they were listened to by the community at large. Even at grass-roots level the local vicar was one
of the most respected members of the village. Not so now! The
church, more often than not, is seen as an out of touch and out
of date institution that commands little respect. Church leaders
no longer hold sway in the community, as they once did, and
the church as a whole makes little impact on the moral conscience of the nation. In short, the church has slowly lost its grip
on society.

Postmodern Dangers

Bearing in mind the postmodern shift which has been taking
place in our culture, there are some particular dangers that I
believe we need to look out for in the future. These mistakes, if
made, will potentially be as catastrophic as the mistakes of the
past have been. One issue that features large in a postmodern
society is the abandonment of any concept of truth. As we have
seen, for many people it does not matter whether or not an idea
or belief is true as long as it is enjoyed by the person who
believes it. In that sense everyone can hold onto their own truth
and not feel threatened by others, because all ideas or beliefs are
considered equally true.

Within the church in recent years there has often been the ten-
dency to downgrade truth in deference to the views and opinions of others. As a theology lecturer, I have sometimes been
accused of fostering division because of my insistence that the
Bible is true and its truths are non-negotiable. Some Christians

have even suggested to me that the study of theology actually dampens spiritual ardour and prevents Christians from simply enjoying their relationship with God. When I hear these views espoused it becomes clear to me that some Christians have indeed imbibed postmodernity into their Christian experience. Whether or not our culture denies the existence of absolutes, the fact is that they do exist. God, who is the ultimate reality, has revealed himself in scripture, and every word is inspired, true and to be believed.

If the church refuses to build its life and existence on the sure foundation of scripture, if we do not insist that truth exists and must be lived out, then the consequences will be dire indeed. We will end up with a church that believes nothing and is willing to compromise on anything for the sake of harmony. Such a church will not be in a position to call people out from the crowd to follow Jesus because it will have blended in with the crowd and will have become indistinguishable from it. Christian doctrine is essential because it is the truth that separates us from those who do not follow Jesus Christ or live a God-honouring lifestyle, and this by definition is what it is to be holy. To water down our doctrines, to treat them as though they are negotiable, is to state that we no longer want to be a holy people acting as salt and light in this dark world.

Furthermore in a postmodern society where everybody's opinion is valid, society is fragmented and divided into a series of 'taste communities' each with its own beliefs and ways of doing things. There is no sense of continuity or overarching ethos that binds us together. Again, some churches are falling for this idea that everyone within the church should be allowed to express his own spiritual life in his particular way. Such churches create different types of church services for the different taste groups within their congregation.

In practice this means that those who enjoy lively worship will go to the lively services while those who are naturally more sombre will go to the more sedate services. While there is need for variety within the life of the church and it is valid for the differing needs of people to be met at an appropriate level (for example teaching done in an all-age Sunday school), there must nevertheless be a tangible expression of the body of Christ within the local congregation. God did not just call lively people to repentance, or people who enjoy a particular type of music. God

called young, old, sedate, energetic, doleful and expressive people to repentance. It is not God's intention to divide us into different 'taste groups', but to unite us by his Spirit into a community where love, tolerance and mutual respect reign. It is precisely when I worship with other Christians who have different
personalities and outlook from myself that Christ is glorified by
our oneness in his name.

Postmodernity is also based on feelings and not facts. It is the
experience and not the reality that counts. Something is said to
be good if it feels good. Logic, rationality and objective right and
wrongs are ditched in favour of what can be enjoyed. Once
again the church is in danger of swallowing the dangerous drug
of postmodernity. When worship is judged by how it makes the
worshipper feel as opposed to the extent of consecration in the
life of the worshipper, then worship has sold out to postmodernity. When biblical exposition and deep theological thinking are
replaced by interesting stories and entertaining presentations,
then postmodernity has entered the pulpit. I am not suggesting
that our worship should be devoid of emotion and our preaching dull. Quite the reverse. I am just as concerned when worship
is no more than a cerebral exercise. For that is modernity, not
Christianity. I am also very much in favour of creativity when
preaching. But there must be substance as well as well as sound-
bite. Otherwise superficiality will rule.

This having been said, it will also be important that we
engage in meaningful dialogue with people. The environment
that people are increasingly coming from is one in which questioning rather than certainty is common. The rejection of
absolutes has led to the need for dialogue and working things
through. This often results in questions being left unanswered
and loose ends left untied. For Christians who like being dog-
matic about their beliefs and who like to have their theology
highly systematised and neatly packaged this is a difficult thing
to handle. They associate questions with unbelief and therefore
take a dim view of the questioner.

Stuart Murray suggests that churches in our postmodern
world need to be 'communities where doubts can be expressed
without fear or censure, where people can explore their uncer-
tainties, rather than toeing the party line'[12]. He notes that

---

12 Murray, *Church Planting*, p.185

Thomas was not rejected when he doubted the resurrection of Christ, but was nurtured back into a position of faith. This policy may have its dangers and may be an uncomfortable thing to live with, but given the uncertainty and doubting that so pervades our society, there seems little alternative. We need to be able to embrace people as they make their first tentative steps towards faith and be willing through nurturing to build up their faith while allowing them a sense of belonging in the church community. Young Christians, and even those who have yet to commit themselves to Christ, need to feel that they can raise issues and express doubts without feeling alienated or rejected. My own experience of Christianity is that I have been able to grow and develop as a Christian despite at times having major questions that I struggled to find answers to.

Questions

1 Why do you think Christianity is growing so rapidly in Latin America and parts of Africa, while in much of the West it appears to make no progress?
2 What evidences are there in your area of the decline of the church?
3 What practical steps can we take to counter liberalism, denominationalism, and isolationism in the life of the church?
4 What will be the end result if the church ceases to preach the authority and centrality of scripture in the life of a believer?
5 To what extent should we gear our church services to the 'personal tastes' of our audience, and what parameters (if any) should govern this decision?

5

Evangelism that Challenges, not Threatens

Having considered where our culture is going and the crisis that affects the church, we now need to think about how we communicate the Christian faith to our community. To do this we need to begin by reminding ourselves about the kind of society we live in and think through the problems that will confront us as we present the gospel.

I concluded the second chapter by stating that the society to which we have been sent believes that God is irrelevant, that scripture carries no authority, that all religions are equally true, that morality is about personal choice and that experience is everything. In the third chapter I tried to outline something of the change that our society is going through, and then in the fourth chapter I tried to make the point that the church in the UK is a relatively small institution that has little impact on national life and that Christianity is a minority interest. What problems will the church face as it communicates the gospel to our society?

Convicting Without Criticising

The first obstacle that we need to cross is people's ambivalence towards sin. In a world where morality has been relativised, the idea of sin is hard to get across. Most people will have some sort of moral code, but it will be reduced to the lowest common denominator so that the only sins are those that hurt others or hurt nature. It will be essential to communicate that other things, such as impure thoughts and improper speech, are sin. The only way to do this is to demonstrate that God is creator and therefore we as his creatures are morally accountable to him. God has objective standards to which we as human beings

are expected to comply. We may not agree with God's standards, but it is he who sets them, not we. Our job is to obey, and
as a human race we have failed to do so.

The communication of this message presupposes that we
have had the opportunity to talk to our non-Christian friends at
some length. The problem is that, as the previous chapter has
indicated, most non-Christians never go to church or engage in
meaningful spiritual dialogue with Christians. Later on I will
deal with how we get alongside non-Christians to share this
message, but for now it is important that we take on board this
important issue. We need to learn how to convince people of the
seriousness of their sin without appearing to criticise them or
cause offence.

Hurdling Pluralism

Another obstacle, which will arise when we communicate
something of the Christian faith, centres around the Christian
belief in the uniqueness of Christianity. The words of Jesus are
clear, 'I am the way, the truth and the life, no one comes to the
Father but by me' (John 14:6). The problem is that in a pluralist
culture such claims of uniqueness are perceived as arrogant and
extremely offensive. Often when I have been speaking to non-
Christians about the Christian message they have replied, 'Well
what about Muslims and Hindus? Are they not going to heav-
en?' The difficulty is that if I were to say, 'No' I would be brand-
ed an offensive bigot, but if I say, 'Possibly' I cease to be true to
what the Bible teaches.

This is a difficult question, but it is one which will frequently
confront us if we are serious about evangelism. We need to learn
how to communicate the truth of the gospel without being offensive about other faiths. I am not suggesting that we capitulate to
the pluralist culture in which we live, far from it. There is only
one way to God and no true Christian can deny that. Our presentation of the gospel must leave people in no doubt that Jesus is
the only way to God. But we must bear in mind the cultural sen-
sitivities of those to whom we witness and tread with caution.

Cerebral Christianity

A third obstacle will be the cerebral nature of Christianity. The

Christian faith is based on certain historic facts, and it is true because these facts are true. However, many in our society are so experience-orientated that they will be turned off by a gospel presentation that relies solely on fact. People are not just looking for something to believe in but also something that they can experience. Christianity will appeal to many in our society only if it is seen to work.

I am conscious that so often my evangelistic preaching depends on a dry presentation of information that feeds the mind but does little else. Very often when I do this someone will say to me, 'But do you enjoy being a Christian? Does it help you live life better?' The person is not disputing the facts that I have presented, he is more interested in the difference that Christianity will make to his life experientially.

Again I am not suggesting that the facts of the Christian faith are irrelevant. Indeed I find Christianity satisfying because, amongst other things, I know it to be true. But Christianity needs to be felt! For all the dangers in an experience-based faith it is important for me, and I suspect every Christian, that my faith makes a difference to my home life, my work life and my social life. Psalm 34:8 says, 'Taste and see that the Lord is good'. The psalmist, having personally experienced God's power in his life, invites others to do so too[1]. As we communicate the gospel to our experience-orientated generation we need to demonstrate that Christianity is not only objectively true, but that it also makes life qualitatively better. Jesus can help a person's marriage, make his life more fulfilling and meaningful, and bring him into the experience of knowing God.

Biblical Illiteracy

A fourth obstacle that we face will be that of biblical illiteracy. Because Christianity has been so marginalised in western society, and because the Bible is not treated with any sense of reverence, for most people the Bible is a book to which they have never turned. If the average man in the street owns a Bible it will probably be gathering dust in some remote cupboard. More likely he will never have owned a Bible and will rarely have heard it quoted.

---

1   Craigie, *Psalms 1-50*, (WBC vol.19), p.279

I find it intriguing when I watch TV quiz shows to see how badly even well educated people handle biblical questions. Recently on 'The Weakest Link' a man was asked which Bible book comes after Genesis. Clearly he had no idea and so mentioned the only other Bible book he knew, which was Revelation. I smiled smugly because having come from a Christian family I could have correctly answered that question at the age of five. But that lack of knowledge of the Bible is not uncommon. Indeed I suspect that most people in the UK would not have been able to name another Bible book.

When it comes to evangelism in this culture, the lack of biblical knowledge will be a big barrier. We will need to find a way of communicating meaningfully to people who know virtually nothing about God, the origin of sin or the person of Jesus Christ. We will need to assume nothing and get into the habit of starting any conversation at the basics.

A Model for Evangelism

How do we begin to communicate the gospel in such an environment? What should be our starting point? Perhaps the most helpful lessons I have learned have been derived from the techniques of some of the biblical evangelists. The foremost of them was Paul and the book of Acts reveals a great deal about his evangelistic strategy. One of the most influential passages for me has been Acts 17:26-38 which records Paul's experience in Athens. I will mention it briefly now and then develop it further later on.

We need to remember, of course, that the culture Paul was dealing with in Athens was a very different one to that of the United Kingdom, but as Don Carson points out, there are also some striking parallels[2]. To begin with, the Athenian culture was pluralistic and a far cry from a Judeo-Christian world view. What is more, in Athens Paul was addressing a group of people who were utterly biblically illiterate and therefore knew absolutely nothing about the God of the Bible.

The first thing to note is Paul's assessment of the culture. Luke tells us that Paul perceived the city was *'full of idols'* (v.16). Considering the kind of city that Athens was this is a remark-

---

2   Carson, *The Gagging of God*, p.496

able observation indeed. Athens reached its heyday under Peri-
cles (495-429 B.C.) and then declined as a military power, finally being conquered by the Romans in 146 BC[3]. Nevertheless it
was a world-famous city, renowned for the splendour of its
buildings, statues and monuments, and as a place of learning.
Athens had been no less than the intellectual capital of the
world. Of the ancient world's three great university cities,
Athens, Tarsus and Alexandria, Athens was the most presti-
gious[4]. It was the home of the great dramatists and philosophers, the cutting edge of culture and education. Into this great
city came Paul. He was not overawed by the grandeur of the
architecture, nor was he taken in by the highly developed cultural life or the sophisticated philosophy, though all of these
were impressive[5]. Rather, he became deeply distressed by the
fact that these people were fallen and idolatrous.

We, too, need to learn to critique the culture in which we live
and view it through Christian eyes. It is easy for people living in
the West to associate the mission field with parts of the world
like Africa and the Far East. Certainly in these places there are
great needs. Sometimes, however, we can become so absorbed
with the technology, education and the cultural sophistication of
the West that we forget that in reality people in the West are per-
missive, idolatrous and morally decadent. The impetus for
evangelism comes as we critique our own culture with Christian eyes and see how spiritually desperate it really is.

Notice also that Paul begins to witness in the synagogue, as
was his custom, but then goes out into the *'market place day by
day'* (v.17) to witness to those who were there. The reason for
this is obvious. Only a few Athenians were likely to enter the
synagogue, so if Paul confined his evangelism to the synagogue
he would only reach the few. To reach the many he had to get
out to the market place. The market place was the centre of public and business life; therefore the most likely place to meet people[6].

In much the same way, we need to think about our market
place and how we can begin to rub shoulders with people in

---

3   Longenecker, *Acts*, p.269
4   *Illustrated Bible Dictionary*, p.147
5   Stott, *The Message of Acts*, p.277
6   Larkin, *Acts*, p.252

natural situations. Bearing in mind that only 7% of people in the United Kingdom attend church, the 93% who remain will need to be reached in some way other than a church service. If the majority of people are to be reached we need to stop thinking of evangelism as being something that is done in a church service and begin to think of it as something that is done 'outside' of the church building.

Paul's Message

Once Paul aroused some interest he was invited to present his case at the Areopagus which was the chief court and main administrative body in Athens[7]. His address shows how he communicated the gospel message. Paul begins by noting that the Athenians are *'very religious'*. He was not complimenting them for their religious beliefs; indeed patronising comments used to win an audience were not tolerated in the Areopagus[8]. Rather he was beginning to build a thought bridge between the biblical position and theirs by establishing some common ground. In short, he was being sensitive and courteous so that he would be in a position to bring the gospel to them[9].

The same kind of presentation is required today. With all the confusion and doubt which our culture is causing, it is simply not tenable to proclaim the gospel from a distance. Preaching at people will not communicate the gospel, it will simply alienate them and heighten the sense that we are different. Rather, we need to establish some common ground which will then lead to the presentation of the gospel.

Not long ago, I was talking to a young man on the streets of Copenhagen where I was preaching in the open air. From the outset of the conversation, it was clear to me that he was full of doubts about God and struggled to believe in any absolutes. Rather than condemn his sceptical world view I built a bridge to his position. I made the comment that he seemed to be struggling with the Christian message and its intellectual credibility. Then I told him that I had experienced many doubts about

---

7   Gill, *The Book of Acts in its First Century Setting*, Vol.2, Ed. D Gill & C
      Gempf, p.447
8   Bruce, *The Book of Acts*, p.355
9   Bruce, *The Book of Acts*, p.499

Christianity before becoming a Christian, and that even as a
Christian I went through times of doubting the accuracy of the
Bible and biblical history. This surprised him, but increased his
interest. We then talked about some of the areas where we were
most liable to be sceptical, for example the historicity of the resurrection. The bridge between us was beginning to be constructed. I then told him that I was now completely satisfied
with my Christian faith because many of my most troubling
doubts had been answered. This simple technique not only
enabled me to go on to explain what I believed, but why I
believed it. In short I was able to share the gospel with him and
explain why the gospel is intellectually credible and defensible.

Having established this bridge, Paul then mentions the altar
to *'an unknown god'* (v.23). This kind of altar was common in
Athens so Paul's audience would easily have identified with
what he was saying[10]. He uses this inscription as a means of
introducing to them the true God who is unknown to them[11].
This was a powerful object lesson and demonstrates one of the
reasons why Paul was so successful as an evangelist. It was
because he spoke their language. He ensured that he presented
God to them in a way that they could understand.

This is something else that Christians need to learn. It does
not take long for someone who goes to church to pick up a great
deal of jargon. So much of the vocabulary and so many of the
expressions that Christians use are incomprehensible to people
who are unchurched. We get so used to using this religious jargon that we do not even realise we are doing it. It is vital, therefore, that we find object lessons and modes of expression that
will enable us to communicate the gospel to our peers so that
they fully understand what we are saying to them.

One of the exercises I set my students is to write out their testimony and a short gospel presentation without using a list of
the words that I write up on the board. Included on this list of
'banned' words are sin, saved, born-again, faith and cleansed.
These words are perfectly good and convey a great deal to
someone who is a Christian, but to someone who is unchurched
they will simply be confusing. Even Jesus had to define what he
meant when his use of the expression born-again confused

---

10   Bruce, *The Book of Acts*, p.271
11   Marshall, *Acts*, p.286

Nicodemus, a leading theologian. To someone who no longer believes in absolutes, the whole concept of sin will require explanation.

Next Paul goes on to explain who the true unknown God is. He deals with the issue of creation (v.24), establishes the fact that we as human beings are accountable to God, and asserts that God wishes a relationship with us (v.27). But then the crunch comes in verse 30! Having built bridges and ensured that he is speaking in their language, Paul ultimately had to challenge the false notions held by the Athenians. They were idolaters and this needed to be dealt with. Though Paul was preaching in a culture that was highly pluralistic, he did not succumb to it.

I believe that Christians need a great deal of courage today if they are to truly communicate the gospel in our pluralist and relativistic society. Though we need to demonstrate love, understanding and grace as we interact with our non-Christian friends, this should never be at the expense of presenting the uniqueness of Christianity. Ultimately the only way of getting to heaven is through the person of Jesus Christ, and those to whom we witness need to know this. We need to hold our nerve and insist, gently but unwaveringly, that salvation comes only as a result of Christ's work on the cross. Paul knew when to play the diplomatic card and when to dig his heels in and contend for the truth, and this is a skill that we need to develop in our witnessing.

It is also significant to note when Paul brings Jesus into his message. What Luke records for us is obviously an abbreviated version of Paul's sermon. Paul talks about God as creator and builds an entire biblical world view before he mentions the person of Jesus Christ. This might seem strange, as the gospel is about Jesus and his death on the cross. But there are reasons for Paul speaking in this way. Suppose he had begun his sermon with the statement, 'Jesus Christ is the Son of God'. This is a perfectly good theological statement that we as Christians know to be true. The trouble is that his audience would not have had the capacity to understand what this meant. Someone in the crowd may well have shouted back, 'OK but of which god is he the son?' Coming from their perspective these people had no idea of who God was, therefore anything which Paul might have said about Jesus would have made very little sense. Jesus and his death on the cross is meaningless without a knowledge of God, man in his relationship to God, the fall, and the incarnation. The Athenians knew nothing of this, and so Paul had to do some preparatory work before coming to the climax of his message, which was obviously God's answer in Christ.

In much the same way, we need to be careful about our assumptions. In a postmodern world where people do not go to church or have any consciousness of personal sin, even sound theological statements will not register because the foundation is not in place. Many of the evangelistic Bible study booklets that I have used over the years are based on the assumption that the users will have a Judeo-Christian worldview. This is increasingly unlikely to be the case. Many unchurched people do not have the faintest idea what the Bible teaches about God and his world. That being the case, John 3:16 and other verses that we use in evangelism may not be enough. A better method of communicating the gospel might be to start by using the book of Genesis to build up a foundation upon which verses like John 3:16 can then make sense.

Don Carson tells the story of a missionary friend who went to India[12]. After his language study he spent a decade travelling around numerous villages preaching the gospel. Many people made professions, but they were only adding Jesus to the long list of deities that they were already worshipping. No churches were planted and few made any real commitment to God as he was unable to break through the deep-rooted pluralism of Indian society. Following a furlough in which he did a lot of soul-searching, he returned to India to concentrate on just two villages. This time he began with the doctrines of God, humanity and the fall. The result was quite different. There were fewer professions, but two churches were planted. The difference was that on his second time round he made no assumptions and built a foundation for belief. This, it seems to me, is exactly what we need to do in our pluralistic society in Britain.

Questions

1 How do we achieve a balance between being relevant in our culture and at the same time not compromising our faith? Give some practical examples.

---

12 Carson, *The Gagging of God*, p.502

2 How can we demonstrate to people that their world view is wrong and that they are sinful, without alienating and offending them?
3 How can we convince people that Christianity is not just a dry and cerebral faith?
4 Paul went to the 'market place' to share his faith. What 'market places' do you have to share your faith in, and what potential 'market places' could you create for evangelism?

6

Up Close and Personal
(The Qualities of a Soul Winner)

Having thought about some of the issues involved in evangelism, we now need to think about the kind of people we need to be if we are to be effective evangelists. The reason for this is obvious. If evangelism is based on relationships and getting alongside people to share the good news, then our lives will be on view to those to whom we are witnessing. People in our postmodern world will not be impressed merely by the message being given to them, but will need to see the message being lived out in the lives of Christians. It is not sufficient in this experience-orientated culture to communicate the facts of the gospel: Christianity must be seen to work and make a difference. This can be done only if we as Christians are living our lives correctly in front of our unchurched friends.

Absence of Hypocrisy

The first thing that we need to ensure is that the life we lead is consistent with the faith we claim to hold. People are not stupid. If we do a lot of talking but do not back it up with a genuinely Christian lifestyle, we will be completely unconvincing. My experience of 'friendship evangelism' is that the people to whom I am witnessing get to know me very well indeed. Therefore putting on a mask of Christianity will not work. My life must be consistent, through and through. As someone wisely commented to me, 'A man's pious words carry no weight if his behaviour is inconsistent with them.'

On each side of the border between North and South Korea there is a military barracks to keep out unwelcome visitors. On the south side, this barracks consists of a few humble buildings. On the communist north side is a glorious and very large building that can be seen for many miles. The reality, however, is that the building is no more than a facade. Viewed from the side it goes back no more than a couple of metres. Christians can live such a sham. Their Christianity is only skin deep. This kind of lifestyle impresses no one and will do irreparable damage to the cause of Christ. In Romans 2:21-24 Paul criticised the Jews for their hypocrisy, stating that the Gentiles were blaspheming God as a result. It was ironic that it was people who claimed to follow God who were the ones who dishonoured God's name, rather than those who did not believe in God[1]. Christians can cause their non-Christian friends to become cynical about the Christian faith if they are inconsistent. On the other hand, a life that displays Christlikeness (Gal. 5:22,23) will earn respect.

A Living Relationship With Christ

The second thing that we need to ensure is that we have a living and active relationship with Jesus Christ. It is said that you become like the company you keep. This is certainly the case with me. I come from Belfast, but have been living near Glasgow for the past twelve years. Over that time my accent has slightly moderated without my even realising it. I have begun to use expressions that are thoroughly Glaswegian and sometimes even say them with a slight Scottish lilt. When I take a short trip back to Ireland my Belfast accent returns with full force. Again it is because of the company I keep.

The same thing applies to the spiritual life, which is why Christian fellowship is so important. In our relationship with Christ, if we spend quality time with him it shows in our life. People can see a perceptible change in our attitudes and conversation. This demonstration of Christlikeness will be an invaluable asset in evangelism because it shows those people we are trying to reach what a change Christ can make in a person's life. I remember visiting a woman in our area who was not a Christian. During our conversation she began to talk about the marvellous change that had taken place in the life of one of her neighbours. It so happens that he was a member of my church, which pleased me no end. She saw in him the difference that God can make in the life of an individual, was greatly impressed

---

1   Moo, *The Epistle to the Romans*, p.166

and thought positively about the Christian faith as a result.

There are other reasons why this living relationship with Christ is so important. For a start, you cannot encourage others to commit themselves to a relationship with Jesus Christ if that is not your own day-to-day experience. It is the reality of our relationship with God that is so convincing. During times when we can't answer all the questions that are put to us it is our living testimony that adds weight to our claims. Though we should not run away from the intellectual challenges brought against Christianity, the reality of what Christ has done in our lives this week is just as convincing an argument.

What is more, a life that is transformed by God is a very attractive one. I well remember the reason why I became a Christian. Although I knew I was a sinner and had heard many convincing presentations of the Christian message, this knowledge formed only a small part of the reason why I made my commitment. The main reason was the lovely Christlikeness I saw in the lives of other Christians. I had the great privilege of coming into contact with a group of young Christians who were deeply spiritual and fun to be with. The reality of their faith could be seen in everything they did and I found myself wanting what they had. It was from this point that I made a commitment to Christ that enabled me to experience all the joy which these role models had. Their Christlikeness proved to be like a magnet drawing me to Christ himself.

The fact is that in much the same way as a bad Christian can turn people off Christianity, a good one can make people want to become Christians. This can only happen when we really are walking closely to Christ and allowing his qualities to rub off on us.

Integrity

Part of Christlikeness is having personal integrity. This is such an important point that it merits a category of its own. I have a friend who is a pastor. When I first met Bob and saw him in action, it made me wonder what qualified him to have such a high profile and responsible position within the church. He is not the best preacher I have ever heard, indeed on the rare occasions that I have heard him I found his style to be a little boring. What is more, he displays very few leadership qualities. Certainly he is a caring man and that is a great quality to have in the Christian service ministry, but he simply does not have the charisma or strength of character to make his ministry dynamic.

Then one day while having a conversation with one of Bob's friends I discovered the reason for his esteemed position within the church. His friend told me that Bob was someone who was utterly trustworthy. He was a man of such integrity that Christians and non-Christians alike would trust him with their lives. Whenever Bob spoke people listened, not because he was a great orator or persuasive debater, but because whatever he said was the truth, the whole truth, and nothing but the truth.

When our non-Christian friends see how we live and hear what we say they will form opinions of us. If we have given the impression that what we say needs to be questioned, or if our actions don't match what we profess to believe, then they will find it more difficult to accept the gospel. If, on the other hand, they find that we are utterly trustworthy, then when we begin to share our faith with them they will be compelled by their own estimation of us to listen carefully to everything we say.

Peace in Crisis

A final quality we will need, if we are to be effective witnesses, is the ability to be at peace even in a time of crisis. We live in a world of change and uncertainty. Many people struggle to cope with all the implications of change. For many people life is about frayed nerves and troubled minds. On top of the struggles of modern existence are the personal crises that many people have to face. Someone loses their job, a teenagers goes off the rails and gives his parents sleepless nights. A sudden death brings devastation to a family, illness brings almost unbearable stress. These crises are commonplace and affect nearly everyone at some point or other.

For Christians, too, life can have its painful moments. But the difference for us is that we have a relationship with the God who controls, not only our lives, but the universe as well. A God who is loving, merciful and wants to help us through all the difficulties that life forces us to confront. David wrote Psalm 3 when he was facing overwhelming odds as his son Absalom rebelled against him[2]. Even though there seemed no way out of

---

2   Craigie, *Psalms 1-50*, (WBC vol.19), p.73

the situation, David was still able to sleep calmly through the night without being afraid of the terrors that would confront him when he woke up the next morning[3]. This was because his faith was real and alive. It sustained him during his moments of crisis.

This kind of reliance on God demonstrates the reality of the Christian faith. As friends observe us not only in the good times, but the bad times as well, they can see the hidden strength that a relationship with God can bring. When Christians who are suffering or going through some kind of trauma are able to rejoice and remain positive, it makes an indelible impression on those who see what is going on. This sense of calm begs the question, why? Why are Christians so positive when their lives are sometimes so awful and full of suffering? These situations enable us as Christians to witness and talk about God's sustaining power, and our words are given credibility by our actions in a time of crisis.

Questions

1 Which of the qualities mentioned in this chapter do you find the most difficult to exhibit in your everyday life and why?
2 What practical steps can you take to overcome this difficulty?
3 What other qualities do you think an evangelist should exhibit and why?

---

3   Leupold, *Exposition of Psalms*, p.63

7

Church-based Evangelism

As we look out onto the cultural landscape of our communities, we need to ask a number of important questions. The first and most basic question is, how will we actually reach people? The answer to this is not a simple one. But we can begin by identifying two basic methods of evangelism. The first of these is church-based evangelism. This could be defined as a method of reaching people using church facilities and an organised group of church members. Simply stated, church-based evangelism seeks to reach people with events that centre on a corporate presentation of the gospel, with the church taking a high profile.

There are many church activities that fit into this category. These include family services, youth and children's clubs, Sunday school, discovery courses, one-off evangelistic events and friendship outings. Each of these church-based evangelism methods can be very useful, but only when they are carefully thought out. I believe it would be worth writing a whole chapter on each of these methods, but space does not permit. Instead I just want to list them, adding brief comments on the issues that we will encounter if we organise them, and tentatively suggesting ways in which we can make the most of them. I do not claim to be an expert in any of these areas; but my comments stem from observations I have made as I have seen others successfully utilising these methods in evangelism.

Family Service

The most basic example of a church-based activity is a family service. Most churches use family services as a major part of their evangelistic strategy. Certainly family services have much to commend them. They provide a welcoming atmosphere which enables visitors to feel relaxed and at ease. The main lim-

itation is that, of necessity, people need to come to a church service to hear the Christian message. No matter how friendly a
church might be or how persistent its members are as they invite
friends, the reality is that only a small proportion of people will
ever come to a service like this. It is for this reason that family
services must form part of a wider strategy rather than being the
main outreach of a church. Given these limitations, however,
family services still have their place within the evangelistic
strategy of most churches.

When family services are planned a number of very basic
questions need to be asked. First, how often should a church
hold a family service? This question is actually quite important
and the answer is less obvious that one might think. As most
churches are accustomed to thinking about church services on a
weekly basis, they automatically assume that their family service must be a weekly event. There is nothing wrong with this
and if a church finds that a significant number of non-Christians
come on a weekly basis, then there may well be good reason for
holding it weekly. But there are other considerations that might
need to be brought into the equation. If, for example, a church
struggles to get people in the community to attend weekly family services, it may be wiser to have them less frequently and put
more effort into inviting people to attend.

In my own church, the Viewpark Christian Fellowship, we
hold what we call 'guest services' only six times per year. If they
were held more frequently we would not be able to put in the
work required to get people in our area attending. We also link
these services with special times of the year such as Remem-
brance Day and Christmas so that they become special occasions for the community. This certainly works for us and we
have found that we get far more people at these occasional services than we would do were they to be held weekly.

Another question that needs to be asked is how the service
should be structured. Discussions might need to take place as to
whether or not communal singing should be part of the programme and whether there should be any preaching. Again
these issues are important and there needs to be a rationale
behind everything that is done during a family service. It is the
shop window of the church and will leave all visitors with an
impression of what the church is like.

My personal preference is for both communal singing and

preaching, though not very much of either. I like communal singing because, although it will be alien to unchurched people, it is nevertheless an important part of the lives of Christians and by including it potential converts are introduced to an aspect of Christian living. My commitment to preaching within a family service stems from my conviction that it is still a method of communication, which if well done, is effective.

Yet another question is what kind of communication methods should be incorporated. This is down to personal choice and resources, but we have found that using video, power point presentations and drama can be very effective in communicating some aspect of the Christian faith. The preaching can then draw everything together and focus the hearer's minds on the challenge of the Christian faith.

Of course all of this presupposes that there will be people in the family service to hear this. As I have travelled around churches in the UK I have often been struck, both by the creativity with which many churches present the Christian faith, and by the lack of hearers. There is little point in putting together an imaginative programme if there is no one to listen for whom the programme has been devised. For many churches, therefore, the main task is to ensure that people actually come to these family services.

There is no simple way of getting unchurched people to come to church. Personally I think that newspaper ads and mass leaflet drops are only of limited value. I suspect that only one person in a thousand will respond to a leaflet and one in ten thousand to a newspaper ad. Certainly that would be average for the area where I live. How then do we get people to attend? One word sums it up – relationships. The kind of people who might come to a family service are those who have some kind of contact with the church. That being the case, if every member of the church would invite colleagues, neighbours and friends to a service, the actual numbers of unchurched people coming to such services would certainly increase. The problem is getting Christians to invite their non-Christian friends. In practice this does not often happen. First, because many Christians have few close non-Christian friends and, second, because Christians often make a strong demarcation between their 'secular life' and their 'church life'. Many Christians are vibrant in church but when they get back to the factory floor or their social circle, they say very little about their faith or church life. This mindset needs to be changed and church members need to make friends with non-Christians. If they were to be more open about their faith and bring it into conversation naturally, they would have a much greater opportunity of bringing others to a family service. However, this whole process will not begin until churches begin to teach their members to be salt and light in their community and to see their non-Christian friends as lost people who desperately need to hear the gospel.

In addition to these relationship contacts it is possible for churches to develop further contacts with people in the community. In my church we have several youth and children's clubs. Most of the young people who attend come from unchurched families, but as they come along to our clubs a contact with their families already exists. A few people in our church sat down and thought about how we should develop this contact. The first thing we did was to visit these homes, 150 in all, and offer them the Jesus video on loan. Because they knew about the church through the clubs, a high percentage of these families took the video and many said that they enjoyed it. We then began to produce a monthly church bulletin that contained details of all the church activities as well as a thought for the month. Each month a group of people from our church visit each of these homes with the bulletin. We employ a friendly, non-threatening approach. The purpose of these visits is not to preach the gospel to the people, though if conversations arise naturally we make the most of them, but rather to develop the contact and show a friendly face. These visits have enabled us to get to know some of the families well and this has resulted in many of them coming to our guest services. This is just one way of developing contacts. The point is not how a church builds relationships, but that it does, and that it is able to bring non-Christians to the family service.

Age-centred Clubs

Another form of church-based evangelism that is widely used is what could be described as age-centred clubs. The most common forms of this are children's and youth clubs, though senior citizens' clubs are also fairly common. Obviously the different age groups represented will determine the kind of club that is formed, but the basic ingredients tend to be the same. A mix of social activity and spiritual input.

Generally speaking most churches do very well when it comes to children's clubs. Even small churches with little gift and few resources can successfully run them. It is more common for churches to struggle with clubs for teenagers, young adults and for people in their thirties and forties. Each of these is quite specialised and needs to be thought through carefully, but I will make a few general remarks about them all.

One of the problems of conducting a youth club is that there is a high casualty rate of young people even before they get to their teenage years. They may have attended the children's club, but because they do not have a relationship with the leaders of the youth club, they simply do not go. This gap has to be bridged. It can be done either by leaders being involved in both clubs or by a half-term feed in between the two clubs. Perhaps both need to be considered. Certainly there needs to be a strategy that links all the clubs being run so that no one falls between them.

Youth clubs can be difficult to run because teenagers like to express themselves, thus often creating discipline problems. It may well be that accountability and discipline need to be thought through. If not, the club will involve a great deal of policing and not much communicating the gospel. Incentives are also useful. In one of the clubs that I work with, we take the young people on outings, for example going to a football match. These outings both build relationships and provide a motive for good behaviour.

When all is said and done, the most important thing that we can give to young people is scripture. This must be done, and creativity is the key. We have found that if the Bible is presented in an imaginative way using video, drama, discussion and object lessons, it is not difficult to get a group of unchurched teenagers to sit and listen for half an hour. Camps are also useful, as they take young people out of their context and into one that is conducive to hearing the gospel. Again relationships will be of the utmost importance as the leaders role model the Christian life for the young people. Positive role models can be hugely effective in winning young people for Christ.

When it comes to running clubs for people in their twenties and thirties there are a number of major obstacles which need to be overcome. First, life is very busy and pressurised so time is a valuable commodity. If you are a family man with a busy job there is little time for anything else. Many professional people come home exhausted at 7.00 pm and then need to spend some time with their families. Going to some church activity is the last thing on their mind, especially if they have no spiritual interest in the first place. That being the case it may well be unrealistic to think of having a weekly activity. It is also increasingly difficult to reach people the older they get. Life's responsibilities, personal hurts and the general scepticism that pervades our society means that many people will be dubious and, perhaps, even antagonistic towards Christianity by the time they reach their mid-twenties.

On the other hand, there are two factors in contemporary society that will enable churches to get alongside people in this age group. First, our society puts great importance on recreation. The huge proliferation of sports clubs and hobbies is evidence of that. What is more, in this age of depersonalising technology people need to interact and socialise. Both of these factors can be utilised by the church.

One thing that often brings people together, especially men, is sport. Many churches have got involved in football and even a church league as a way of relaxing and enjoying time with non-Christian friends. I and another leader in my church play every week with a group of young men. It would be wrong to say that this gives us regular opportunities to share the gospel. However it does bring us into contact with a group of men who would never darken the doors of a church or think about spiritual things. Our prayer is that the relationships that we build will one day enable us to effectively communicate the gospel to these men in a way that we have never had the opportunity to do before.

But it is not just sport that brings people together. In many churches, craft groups and mother and toddler groups have done much the same thing. Some churches have also successfully organised father and son clubs or mother and daughter clubs. The idea is to develop an activity or hobby that the parents can do with their children. One church that I have worked with had a swimming pool not far from the church building. They began a father and son swimming club that proved to be very popular in the local community, not least because it provided an opportunity for fathers to spend quality time with their sons as well as make new friends.

Again, the gospel will not always be presented in a very upfront way, but the friendships that are developed in these activities will enable the Christians to share the gospel informally with their non-Christian friends. The secret to success in such ventures is developing the knack of gossiping the gospel. When persecution hit the early church, as recorded in Acts 8, the Christians literally had to scatter in all directions. They did not have the time to organise evangelistic events, but what they did do was to 'spread the good news' wherever they went (v.4)[1]. It was this spontaneous evangelism to which the church as a whole committed themselves that contributed to the great success of this evangelistic endeavour. Today, as individual Christians use the opportunities presented to them within any club that the church forms, the gospel is shared without any 'formal' presentation of the truths of Christianity.

Event Evangelism

As well as these regular activities there is a whole range of one-off events that churches can organise in order to make contacts and deepen friendship. In some cases, there may not be a specific evangelistic thrust in these events, but they provide a setting in which Christians rub shoulders with unchurched people and witness naturally. Recently, as a church, we organised a 'paint ball' outing to reach and make contact with unchurched men. It may seem to be an unlikely evangelism event, but it proved very successful. It was the kind of activity that attracts men of all ages and promotes group bonding. We went through a succession of five battle zones with a coffee break in-between. By the end of the evening we had made friends with several unchurched men, some of whom came a few nights later to an outreach meal. During the mock battles we were aiming our paint guns at each other, but the real aim, which was to get to know each other in an informal setting, was constantly at the back of our minds. The evening was a big success and made contacts which we are still following up.

There are many less boisterous events that can have the same

---

1   Stott, *The Message of Acts*, p.146

impact. Some churches organise craft fairs or car boot sales in order to befriend people. Others organise activities in their local school and hold a prize giving in their church during a family service. On a number of occasions I have also been involved in organising an interactive Passover celebration complete with Israeli wine, unleavened bread and roast lamb. These events go down well in our pluralist society, and provide appropriate imagery for communicating the gospel. Sometimes these events can be structured and have a specific aim in mind. Recently in our church we organised a parenting class. Like many parts of the UK, our area has its fair share of one-parent families, and parents who are struggling to bring up their children. We held a parenting class both to reach new people and to offer a service to the community. It was so successful that we have continued it, and these classes have become an important building block in our evangelism strategy. Whatever the event, if it brings Christians into contact with non-Christians in such a way as to develop friendship, and if the Christians are prepared to take every opportunity to gently share their faith, then it will be a success.

Discovery Courses

One last form of church-based outreach that has proved to be successful is the discovery course. Some of these courses, like the Alpha course, are ready-made and can easily be utilised by churches. In some cases, it may be more appropriate for a church to develop its own course. But, however a church may wish to proceed with this type of outreach, it has a proven track record.

This type of event has a number of benefits. First, it brings non-Christians into a Christian atmosphere on a regular basis over a period of time. Second, the time given enables the Christian message to be explained systematically and with clarity. Third, it provides the opportunity for feedback and for any questions and doubts to be dealt with. Fourth, it takes attenders from the stage where they are vaguely interested in Christianity to the point where they are being challenged to make some kind of commitment. Fifth, courses of this kind can evolve naturally into discipleship classes, once someone has made a commitment to Christ.

There are a number of key elements in this type of course.

Those who attend need to feel at home, otherwise they will not keep going until the end of the course. Alpha courses are centred around a meal and this is one reason why they work so well. Eating out is a social activity that enables people to form friendships easily. A meal as part of a church-organised course has the same effect. If there are not the facilities to put on a full meal, finger buffets work equally well. Using a hotel or restaurant may also be an option albeit the cost would be much higher.

There are several important rules to observe when laying on a discovery course. It is important, first, to have people who can competently lead it. These events are informal, but informality can descend into chaos if not well regulated. Second, it is important to ensure that Christians are mingling with non-Christians so that as much can be communicated outside of the 'main talk' as is done during it. Third, deal with any questions and issues that emerge honestly and frankly. And, finally, engender the kind of atmosphere that will make visitors want to come back again and again.

Questions

1 What practical steps can your church take to improve its family service?
2 Think of some events that will draw people towards your church, and discuss how you would get the most out of these events.
3 Imagine you were given the job of writing a 'discovery course' for your church. What would you include and why?
4 Discuss the following statement: 'In today's post-Christian, biblically illiterate society, evangelism needs to be more than just preaching human sinfulness and Christ's saving work, rather it should be a whole process of education in which the recipient is taught the whole Christian worldview'.

8

Friendship Evangelism

Having considered what is involved in church-based evangelism, we will now look at the issues involved in friendship evangelism. This could be defined as individual Christians taking the initiative to share the gospel with their contemporaries. It is a form of evangelism that does not depend on organised church programmes but, rather, involves the informal communication of the gospel by motivated individuals. Some describe this as 'gossiping the gospel'. It is precisely this sort of evangelism that we see so often in the book of Acts.

There are a number of reasons why this kind of evangelism is necessary. First, church-based evangelism presupposes that people who are not Christians will nevertheless come to a church event. Certainly in many cases where Christians have built up a relationship with their non-Christian friends this may well be a possibility. However, the majority of people will not want to come to any event that the church holds. Among the reasons for this is the widely held view that the church is a rather frightening place, full of intolerant people, and its activities are boring and irrelevant. Friendship evangelism, on the other hand, does not require any church-based activities or the use of church premises.

Second, church-based evangelism does not in itself produce many initial contacts. In general, people who come to church-based events already have some kind of relationship with Christians prior to darkening the doors of a church building. They come because their Christian friends have invited them. Leaflet drops and newspaper adverts have a very modest effect on church attendance. The majority of non-Christians who come to a church-based event will have been personally invited. When it comes to friendship evangelism, however, initial contacts are made relatively easily. Christians who are committed to evangelism will make contacts among their friends, neighbours, colleagues and just about anybody they come into contact with.

Third, in order for church-based evangelism to be effective, the people being reached have to be at a certain stage in their spiritual awareness. No matter how user-friendly a church event may be, there will always be a little pensiveness on the part of the person being invited. Unless they are utterly stupid they will be aware that this church wants them to convert and this is a pressure even if it is something they want to do. Friendship evangelism can happen even if the person is nowhere spiritually and has no inclination to become a Christian. The person is not being pressurised. They are simply hearing, in an informal setting, that God loves them and can make a difference in their lives.

Though the two types of evangelism are quite different, they are nonetheless complementary. As Christians make contacts with people who are unchurched, they can develop their relationship to the point where they can involve their new-found friends with some church-based activities. In this way they can get support from other church members to communicate something of the gospel. Friendship evangelism can therefore be seen as a feeder into church-based evangelism.

Some Dangers

Though it is a crucial plank in a church's evangelism strategy, it must be noted that there are some inherent dangers in friendship evangelism. These can be avoided, but only if we are aware of them. The first danger is linked with the fact that to be effective in friendship evangelism, Christians need to make friends with non-Christians and spend time with them. Their positive influence within that circle of people is part of what it means to be salt and light. This relationship-building with people who are not Christians can sometimes result in difficult questions having to be asked. Do I go to the pub with my friends? What should I do when I am asked to go out clubbing? Are there other places I should not go to, or things I should not do when spending time with them? These questions are not easy to answer. Nowhere in the Bible are we told not to go into pubs. That does not necessarily mean that it is permissible, or helpful, but the decision to go or not should be thought about carefully. Personally, I would

suggest erring on the side of caution, as I have known of many
Christians who struggled in their faith because they lacked caution in this area.

This relationship-building with non-Christians should not be
at the expense of Christians spending time with other Christians. It is also important that Christians do not go out of their
depth when engaging in friendship evangelism. It would be
tragic if any became so immersed in a non-Christian atmosphere
that they became absorbed into it. That would not lead to more
converts but rather to fewer committed Christians.

Another danger linked with friendship evangelism is that a
Christian could be positively influencing his friends to think
about Christianity, but with no reference to the church. This is
dangerous because it could ultimately lead to these contacts
thinking that Christianity and church are two different things. I
have heard many people say to me, 'You can be religious without going to church'. In our postmodern society many want to
enjoy their own private spirituality without having the accountability of being part of a local church. We must never give people this excuse. While it might not be wise to invite friends to
church activities after the first conversation about spiritual matters, the church must at some time come into the dialogue. Otherwise there will be conversions but no church growth.

A third danger that can exist is that Christians who are
involved in friendship evangelism can develop very claustro-
phobic relationships with those they witness to. I have sometimes seen Christians bring others to a point of decision and
develop such a close relationship with the people they are witnessing to that they become followers of those who lead them to
Christ as well as followers of Christ himself. Our priority in
evangelism is to focus people's minds on Christ and encourage
them to be loyal to him, not to us. We should not be in the business of evangelism to meet our own emotional needs. It is a task
that must be performed selflessly and with humility.

The Difficulties

As well as these inherent dangers, there are also some difficulties that we need to address as we get involved in friendship
evangelism. First and foremost is the fact that most Christians
have very few non-Christian friends. Each year at Tilsley Col-

lege, I begin my evangelism classes by asking the students to make a list of their ten closest friends. I then ask them to put an asterisk beside the name of any friend on this list who is not a Christian. The results are often very revealing. The majority of students only have a couple of friends on the list who are not Christians. There is also a link between the length of time a person has been a Christian and the number of non-Christian friends, with new Christians having more non-Christian friends. Though some students are better than others at making friends with non-Christians, only a few of my students have a large number of close friends who are non-Christian, and some have none. It is worth noting that all of the students in our college are committed Christians and many go on to the overseas mission field and plant churches around the world. Nevertheless, despite their commitment to evangelism and the extending of God's kingdom, few are good at befriending people who are not Christians.

If this is a problem with highly motivated Bible college students, it will be an even bigger problem in the church. As Christians we have become so withdrawn from the society around us that many of us are simply not in a position to be salt and light. Let me illustrate the problem with a parable.

Mr. Jones has just become a Christian. He is in his early thirties, single, upwardly mobile and has an active social life. Through the witness of some Christians at his place of work, he becomes a Christian and goes to church for the first time. He finds it a strange place, but people are warm and friendly and openly welcome him into their homes. This he enjoys, though his new Christian friends all seem to discourage him from spending too much time with his existing friends. Clearly they are concerned that his 'old' friends will be a bad influence on him and might drag him back into his former lifestyle. Mr. Jones does not fully understand the logic of the situation, but the combined pressure of these well-intentioned church members, and the teaching in church against worldliness, make it hard for him to do otherwise.

In any case, since going to church and socialising with his new Christian friends, Mr. Jones finds that he has little time to mix with his non-Christian friends anyway. The result is that he sees less and less of them until he barely regards them as friends at all. In a few short years he has gone from being in touch with a great many non-Christians at work and in his social life, to having no non-Christian friends at all. Like most of the Christians in his church, he has effectively cut himself off from the very people who desperately need what he has experienced, namely Jesus Christ.

Though parabolic, this has indeed happened in churches all over the country. It is easy to understand why it happens, but this withdrawing from the world in which we live is neither biblical nor an effective policy. It merely builds into the church a siege mentality that makes it more and more difficult to reach out to a dying world.

Another problem that many Christians face is that they do not know how to be natural about their Christian faith. Due to the secular nature of our society, they feel that they have to live a double life. There is the spiritual life where they attend church on a Sunday and read their Bibles in the privacy of their homes. Then there is the secular life where they go to work, chat to their neighbours over the garden fence and socialise. These two lives are not integrated, and they rarely meet. Occasionally some Christians get a conscience about this and feel that they really need to say something spiritual to a non-Christian. They pluck up the courage and go for it. But in their anxiety to say something telling, they shove an indigestible amount of theological information down the throats of their friends and do so with such force that it ends up being counterproductive. Clearly this situation is not good.

A Way Forward

Having noted both the dangers and the difficulties of friendship evangelism we need to think of a way forward. Without the use of friendship evangelism, our evangelistic strategy will be limited to things we can do in a church building. This will seriously inhibit future growth. It is crucial therefore that we learn as churches to mobilise members and involve them in friendship evangelism. This is an area where, for two reasons, church leaders must take the lead. First, because, without their input, many church members will not mobilise themselves to get involved in friendship evangelism, and second, because, without this programme being strategically led from the front, there will be little by way of training, coordination or support for those who engage in evangelism.

There are various stages in the process of moving people out into friendship evangelism. The first of these is education. The need for education cannot be overstated. It is necessary for two reasons. First, many Christians have a false view of their role within society. They have misinterpreted scriptures that talk about Christians being separated from the world. While it is undoubtedly true that we are to have a distinctively Christian lifestyle that will separate us from the sinfulness of the world in which we live, nowhere in the Bible are we told to cut ourselves off and become spiritual hermits within society. Quite the reverse! We are here to be salt and light in society, and that, by its very nature, involves radiating God's light, and acting as a preservative, in our workplace, neighbourhood and among our friends. As Christians get involved at the very heart of society, as they work honourably in their factories, get involved in politics, and play a full role in civic life, so they bring a Christian presence into all of those situations. In that sense, how we go about every day life is all part of our service to God.

Second, education is necessary because many Christians think that evangelism is someone else's responsibility. This is particularly the case if they belong to a church in which there are active evangelists or the church already has a busy evangelism programme. The average man in the pew thinks that, since evangelism is already happening, he personally does not need to play a role in it. This is not the case, since we are all called to be witnesses whether we like it or not (Acts 1:8). Each member of the church is an ambassador representing God to their friends and neighbours (2 Cor.5:20). Somehow this needs to come through in every church teaching programme.

In my own church, we not only preach frequently on the issue of evangelism, we also find ways of encouraging church members to witness to specific people that they know. One method that we use is to give each church member a 'covenant card'. On this card there is a space to write the name of a person that they know who is not a Christian. The card asks them to make a commitment to pray for this person, to witness to them and to bring them to a church activity. After prayerful consideration, they sign the card as a declaration before God that they will endeavour to follow the obligations that this demands.

As well as educating church members about their responsibilities in evangelism, we also need to train them to evangelise. A number of things should be included in this training. For example, we need to train people to share their faith in an intelligible way, free from religious jargon, and succinctly. It is also very useful to train people to give their 'testimony', that is to share their personal experience of how God has changed their lives.

In addition, we may need to give some training on how to get in touch with people who are non-Christians and how to share the Christian faith in a non-threatening way. Back in chapter five I mentioned the fact that in Athens Paul went out to the marketplace to share the gospel. We need to ask what our marketplace is. In essence it could be any situation where Christians are brought together with non-Christians in a natural setting.

Most Christians already have a marketplace without realising it. Neighbours, colleagues at work and family members are all part of it. We need to train our church members to make the most of opportunities that arise in conversation with these people and to share the gospel naturally where appropriate. But we can also create new marketplaces. In a society where leisure is so highly prized, there are many opportunities to get alongside people to share the gospel. We can encourage church members to join a chess club, a football team, or the local women's guild. All these openings will allow a Christian influence to be felt in many lives and will provide the Christians involved with the opportunity to say something about their faith.

The next stage is to resource the people that have been mobilised for evangelism. This resourcing can take several forms. There are material resources like tracts, Christian books, videos and Bibles. These will prove very useful in the appropriate situations. One friend of mine was witnessing to a man who had many questions about the reliability of the Bible and the truthfulness of Christianity. He was able to give the man a copy of the book *Evidence that demands a Verdict* by Josh McDowell. It proved to be hugely helpful and the man eventually became a Christian. I have also used and recommended everything from videos on apologetics to booklets on bereavement. These resources, if used wisely, can be very powerful indeed.

Another form of resourcing that often gets overlooked is that of spiritual support which includes both advice and prayer. I have already mentioned the fact that Christians can find themselves in difficult situations as they become involved in the lives of those to whom they are witnessing. Friendship evangelism makes us vulnerable to temptation and spiritual attack. Soldiers in the frontline of a battle suffer a high casualty rate. The spiritual battle that rages, when Christians carry the gospel with them, is no less real. Unless we learn to support them and provide them with spiritual back-up they will suffer.

It is important that all the evangelism that is being done is coordinated. There is a sense in which the level of coordination will be dependent on the stage reached and the level of interest being shown. For example, it would be neither feasible nor desirable to coordinate all the many conversations that take place between church members and their non-Christian friends. However, if some of those non-Christians were beginning to show real interest and were asking meaningful questions about the Christian faith, then some measure of coordination would be possible. It might involve the following:

1. Those involved in evangelism could share with members of the church the names of contacts so that others can pray for them. This could be done informally or in a house group or prayer meeting.
2. Leaders could keep in touch with people who are actively involved in friendship evangelism and offer advice and pastoral care.
3. Other church members could be introduced to the contacts in an informal setting so that they too could be a positive influence. Recently a group of people from our church went to the cinema. Several of the group brought non-Christian contacts with them and in this context we were able to get to know those people in a relaxed environment which was a help to those who had made the initial contact. Other church members inviting the person involved in evangelism and their contact to a meal can achieve the same thing.
4. Small prayer groups or prayer triplets could be set up to pray specifically and regularly for contacts.

One final issue that needs to be thought about is how to introduce the person being contacted to the life of the church. It seems to me that a church that is committed to friendship evangelism will also have to put on regular, user-friendly events to which church members can bring their contacts. Bearing in mind that these occasions might be the very first time that the contact has ever been to any kind of church event, they need to be thought through very carefully. The kind of family services or one-off events mentioned in the previous chapter would be ideal.

It is said that first impressions last. To a degree I think this is true. The first experience of a church event will colour the way a non-Christian perceives church. This first meeting must be planned. The responsibility for this lies both with the person who has made the contact and the leadership of the church. The person who has made the contact needs to communicate well with the leadership of the church so that there will be awareness about who is coming to the event. It is also the responsibility of this person to decide what kind of event their friend would be best suited to. Some questions might need to be asked. Is my friend very sceptical about Christianity? Does he find it difficult to mingle in big crowds? Would a more subtle approach be appropriate or is he at the stage where he needs to be challenged about his spiritual condition in an up-front way? These questions will help to determine how the contact should be introduced to the church.

The leaders of the church also have a role to play. They need to ensure that there is a range of events that people could be brought to in the first place. These events could vary from something as unthreatening as a barbeque or a family fun day to something more direct like an evangelistic service. They should also ensure that there will be a warm welcome for visitors. This needs to be stated because it does not always happen. I have often gone into strange churches while on holiday and had the uncomfortable experience of not being welcomed by anyone. Some churches are naturally friendly and have people who find it easy and natural to chat to newcomers, but others do not. In the culture of Viewpark where my church is situated, it would not be a natural thing to walk up to a complete stranger and welcome them. It takes a special kind of person to do this. Church leaders need to ensure that such people are available and ready to do their job. It is helpful to have an actual welcoming team whose job is to befriend people and chat to them as they come into the event. This does not necessarily mean a group of people standing at the church door ready to pounce on people as soon as they walk in. But there must be a structure in place that ensures that every visitor feels at home and cared for.

Questions

1 Discuss the advantages that friendship evangelism has over church-based evangelism.
2 How can a Christian interact socially with non-Christians on the level of authentic friendship, and at the same time maintain a distinctness of life?
3 Discuss practical ways in which a church can encourage its members to get involved in society, and also ways of pastoring them as they do so.
4 What are the issues involved in introducing a person into the life of the local church before they make a personal commitment to Christ?

9

Planning an Evangelistic Strategy

Whether the emphasis of a church's evangelism is focused on church-based evangelism, personal evangelism or both, there is need for an overall strategy. All too often, churches go about their evangelism in a random way without carefully planning how they will reach others. If a church is full of enthusiastic evangelists then there will be an impact, but the effect could be greatly enhanced by careful planning.

But how does a church go about developing a coherent strategy for evangelism? The answer is to do it carefully, methodically and in stages. The task of making disciples is such an important one that no amount of time and effort is too much. We need to work out a strategy that will be effective, and also maintain that effectiveness by continuing to respond to needs that we see around us.

Analysis

The first stage in the process of developing a strategy is to ask the question, where are we now? It is self-evident that if we want to get anywhere, we need to know what our starting point is. Just as a shopping centre map will have an arrow pointing to a red dot stating 'You are here', so we need to find the red dot in our church's evangelism programme.

Analysis is often a very difficult thing for several reasons. First, it is painful. Any honest analysis will reveal flaws and shortcomings in our evangelism and most of us don't like admitting to them. Church leaders, in particular, struggle with this because they often think that a lack of effectiveness in the evangelistic work of their church is a personal reflection on their leadership skills. Though to a degree this might be true, two things must be borne in mind. We need to recognise that all of us are fallible humans and that mistakes and shortcomings are part of life. Recognising this is not tantamount to admitting failure or an excuse for mediocrity; it is merely a recognition that even very good leaders need to work hard at what they do, and that every church can do better. We also need to realize that the salvation of lost men and women is incomparably more important than a bruised ego.

If this process of analysis is to be successful, it must be characterised by rigour, honesty and genuinely penetrating questions. There should be no room for flattery, self-congratulation or excuse. The whole point of an analysis is to discover what is working, what is not working at present, and what will never work. There will be two dangers to look out for. First, there is the danger of sacred cows. By that I mean evangelistic activities to which we have an emotional attachment, but which are ineffective. Second, there is the danger of bypassing successful evangelistic activities without asking whether this activity can be made more successful. If you can avoid these two pitfalls, then your analysis is much more liable to be useful.

What sort of questions do we need to ask in this analysis? It seems to me that there are two types of question. The first type seeks to assess the general spiritual health of the church. Though these questions are not specifically related to evangelism, they are important because churches that are spiritually healthy are more likely to be successful in their evangelism than churches that are not. The second type of question assesses whether the evangelism being done by the church is effective. The following are examples of the first type of question:

1. Is this church committed to Bible teaching?
2. Is this church committed to prayer?
3. To what extent is this church characterised by unity?
4. What commitment is there in this church to worship?
5. To what extent is this church concerned with the glory of God?

Each of these questions must be answered honestly. The answers will indicate whether we are genuinely ready to grow as a church or not. We may get people coming along to our church services, but that is not necessarily growth. Real growth involves people committing themselves to Jesus Christ, and then developing in their spiritual maturity. Remember we are disciple-makers not scalp-hunters.

The second type of question goes further and seeks to determine if our churches are geared up for the specific task of evangelism and disciple making. The following are examples of the kind of question we need to be asking:

1. How successful is this church in reaching out to unchurched people?
2. To what extent are we prepared to be innovative in our outreach?
3. How welcoming of strangers are we?
4. How loved and cared for do church members feel?
5. To what extent are the members of this church mobilized for action?
6. To what extent are members of this church prepared to make personal sacrifices in order to advance the kingdom of God?
7. Are we as a church aware of the spiritual needs of the community?
8. What are we prepared to do to meet those needs?

Without being too harsh I would want to suggest that if your church has a 'low score' on each of these questions, then it is simply not ready to make disciples. A divided, unfriendly, tradition-bound and unwilling church will not be an effective one.

When this analysis has been done, it is important to avoid the twin evils of complacency and negativity. If your church scores highly on these questions, it is easy to feel that things are sufficiently good and rest on your laurels. This is deadly! No matter how well your church is doing, it could always be doing better. It is also possible that at some time in the future your church will be doing less well, so vigilance is never out of place. If, on the other hand, your church does rather badly in relation to these questions you need to avoid despairing. The situation is indeed gloomy, but it can change if there is a will to bring about change. A church is beaten only if its members want to be beaten. With prayer and concerted effort it is possible to turn a church around. Certainly it is better to go through the pain of honest assessment and to change, than to die. Be positive and focus not on where your church is now but on where it could be. Seeing potential and tapping it is one of the secrets of church growth.

Setting Goals

Once the analysis is complete, the next stage is to begin setting goals. It is one thing to discover where you are at present, it is quite another to decide where you want to go. There is an old adage that says that 'If you aim at nowhere, you are bound to get there.' This is quite true when it comes to setting church goals. Unless you determine what you want your church to be like, you will not have any direction to go in. This listless drift will never lead to people becoming Christians and the church growing.

Not only is it important to set goals, you need to set the right kind of goals. This requires careful thought. Too much haste, and your church could end up running hard in the wrong direction. But if the goals you set are the right ones, you can move forward in a united and confident way. Whatever goals you set, they should have the following characteristics:

They Should be Realistic

This sounds obvious, but it is easy to allow enthusiasm to get the better of you and to rush into aiming for goals which you will never be able to achieve. Goals that are not realistic will eventually lead to discouragement when they are not reached. Better to set goals that are reachable and to have the satisfaction of being able to say, 'With God's help we did it.'

By definition, realistic goals are neither overly pessimistic nor hugely optimistic. The balance needs to be somewhere in the middle. For my own church that has a membership of thirty-five, it would be just as mistaken to set a goal of one new member over the next five years as to expect five hundred. Your goal-setting will require both sanctified common sense and belief in the power of God. You may also want to have some interim goals, or goals that are set in stages. This way you can make progress and still be pressing on in the right direction. It also makes it possible to include goals that your church is not presently capable of reaching, but will be at some time in the future.

They Should be Measurable

Again this sounds obvious, but in my experience it is easy to set goals without asking the question, 'How will we know when we have got there?' Goals need to be measurable so that you know

when you have crossed over the line and made those goals part
of history[1]. It is very encouraging to look back and see in con-
crete terms what has been achieved.

Part of the measurement process is having a timescale. Like
the goals themselves, the timescale needs to be realistic. Some
goals might be achieved fairly quickly, while others take some
time. Be careful not to have timescales that demand progress too
soon. Some things will take time to achieve, and patience is necessary. On the other hand don't get used to the luxury of allowing too much time, or the sense of urgency will be lost.

Measurable goals demand specific targets. If you say that
your goal is to do more outreach, that is open to a great deal of
subjective interpretation. It is altogether too vague. It would be
better to have the goal of presenting the gospel to one hundred
people over the next year or to increase church membership by
five people over the next two years. These goals can be meas-
ured in terms of quantity and timescale. Measurable goals lead
to specific achievements, and they give a focus to our efforts.

They Should be Visionary

It is important when setting goals not to underestimate the
potential that your church has when being used by an almighty
God. A friend of mine once said that you should fill church com-
mittees with optimists. I believe this to be at least partly true.
Certainly the people at the forefront of your church should be
visionaries. We have a great God and one who can work powerfully through failing individuals like us. We need to get an
insight into God's vision for our community, and set goals
accordingly.

They Should be Prayerful

Goals should also be prayerfully set. As an elder in a church I
constantly need to remind myself that the church I help to lead
is God's church, not mine. In setting goals for our church we
always need to recognise that God's will is paramount. This is
not an excuse for fatalistic inactivity. Rather we need to seek
God's direction at all times and move forward listening to his
voice.

---

1   Brierley, *Priorities, Planning and Paperwork*, p.32

They Should be Agreed

One final point that needs to be made is that the goals that are set for a particular church should have the consent of the members of that church. Better still, the members need to own the vision. Many leaders are very good at creating ideas and strategies for evangelism, but very poor at bringing the rest of the church along with them. Practicalities dictate that the goals of a church will be decided on by a few, but they should be communicated to the church as a whole and sold in such a way that the church members get excited about them. If the whole church can agree to the goals, the battle is half won.

Determining Methods

Once you have set your goals, the next stage is to decide how those goals can be accomplished. Often churches can be activity-based and feel that they are doing their job because a lot of things are happening. This is not necessarily the case. In fact indulging in excessive activity can be counterproductive. Having lots of activities and then trying to find a rationale for them is a bit like putting the cart before the horse. It is much better to decide what you want to achieve (by setting goals) and then try to find ways of achieving it. Creating an unwieldy monster of activity that is hard to maintain and directionless will not make the most of the resources that your church possesses. Don't create monsters, create well-oiled machines.

The time will inevitably come when you have to slaughter the sacred cows that I mentioned earlier. There are always some activities that simply do not work and so need to be ditched. No church will have enough people to sustain them: they are an unnecessary luxury. The problem is that some of the people involved in these activities will have an emotional attachment to them. This is partly because they have good memories of the days when they did work and partly because they simply enjoy them.

I can remember a youth club that we used to run in my church. It was a lot of fun and most of the leaders enjoyed it, despite the rowdiness of the kids. As the years went by, however, there seemed to be nothing to show for all our work. The youth club did give us credibility in the community and made our church known, but no young people were becoming Christians. Ultimately we had to make changes. The club had served its purpose in establishing contacts with people in the locality, but our new goal was to see young people trust Christ, and the old method was not delivering. It was hard to see the club go, but we began a new one with a new format that was much better suited to the goals that we had set. Be merciless with the sacred cows and the dividends will rapidly become apparent.

As you set about determining the methods that will achieve your goals there are a number of questions you need to ask. They are simple, but they will determine whether or not your methods are appropriate.

Can the Church Wear the Method?

When it comes to the issue of determining methods, it is necessary to be pragmatic and ask if the members of your church will be willing to see this method being used. After all, evangelism and disciple-making is the job of the whole church, not just a few specialists. The more people in your church that get involved the more likely you are to make a real impact. You are therefore reliant upon the support of church members.

Sometimes when it comes to new initiatives, people need a little coaxing. Human beings enjoy routine and therefore need to be convinced that something different is really worthwhile. Often church leaders will be able to sell ideas to their congregation, but not always. It may well be that, at times, discretion is the better part of valour. If that is the case with one of the methods that you propose, perhaps it is better to move on to another method.

Do We Have the Human Resources?

A second practical concern is whether or not you have the people to carry out the proposed method. I have come across many good evangelistic ideas in my travels that require a lot of people to carry them out. In a small church where people are already busy, some of the ideas you might have for evangelism might just be too much for the limited personnel.

Do We Have the Gift?

Even when you have enough people to carry out some evangelistic activity, you still need to ask if you have the right kind of people, or rather the right kind of gifts. Again, I have come across many innovative forms of outreach but they require a special kind of gifting. They may be very effective, but only if the right people to carry them out are available.

Will This Method Achieve the Goals?

This question takes us right back to our goals (which is where we want to be). With every idea that you can think about, you will need to continually refer back to the goals you have set and ask if this method will really work. If not, then don't even think of using it. You will merely be building up your stock of sacred cows just when you want to be depleting it!

Is This the Best Method?

Even when you come across an idea that is likely to work, you still need to ask if it is the best possible method. This will, of course, send you back to the drawing board, but why design something that will have mediocre success when you can have something that will be very successful?

It is important to remember that the right method will always achieve more than the wrong one, so it pays to take the time to get it right. At this point it must be stated that coming up with good methods for reaching people will require a great deal of imagination and creativity. The job of leadership is to lead, but not all leaders will be creative individuals. It is essential that the most creative people in your church are encouraged to come up with methods and initiatives. A lack of creativity is one of my weaknesses. I have no problem talking to people about my faith. To this extent I do believe that I have been given the gift of evangelism. I can communicate my faith coherently and can back up my claims with convincing arguments. But when it comes to dreaming up new ideas for evangelism or finding ways of getting into the community I am not very good. Thankfully there are people in my church who are good at doing this and, as a team, we can be effective. The lesson is clear. We need to use all the gifts that God has given us, and together we will be able to make an impact.

Implementation

Even when you have come up with a series of methods that will achieve your stated goals, the job is still not done. You now have to implement those methods. In my experience this is the most difficult stage in the whole process. It is one thing to excite people in your church with a series of goals and come up with the right methodology; it is quite another to get people doing something. The triple evils of laziness, apathy and fear will conspire against you. The Bible pictures the church as an army ready for battle (Eph.6:10-20) but sometimes local churches are no more than a collection of mavericks and deserters. Getting action out of the 'slumbering saints' and unity among the lone rangers is a tricky job indeed.

But implementing methods is more complex than just rousing the troops. If the methods you are proposing are very different from those already in place then any progress may involve wholesale change. The existing structures may prove inadequate and entirely new structures may need to be put in place. Let me give one simple example. About thirty years ago many independent evangelical churches decided that the Sunday evening evangelistic service was not producing the goods. The main reason for this was that most of the people that these services targeted were in their homes watching TV.

Many of these churches then decided to introduce a morning family service. This was to be the new method of reaching people. The problem was that the church worship service was held in the morning and there was therefore a clash in the programme. In order to facilitate this method, the Sunday programme had to be changed. Some churches did this by moving the worship service to an earlier slot while others moved it to the evening. The reality is that this move split some churches, though the end result was undoubtedly for the best. This is the kind of change that new methods necessitate.

Change is never easy and many churches do not manage change well. Despite this the effort must be made. Without a willingness to change inadequate structures and bring in new ones, the new methods will never make the journey from the drawing board to reality. As you go about restructuring, the need for rationalisation may become apparent. No one church can do everything. However big and talent-laden a church may be, it will always have its limitations. As new structures and methods are put into practice, adding to the overall burdens of the church, something will have to go. You need to ask yourself what the priorities are. A particular activity may be perfectly valid and effective, but if the resources (human and otherwise) are simply not available, then it cannot happen. It is better to do a smaller number of things well than to do more, but do them badly.

Here are a few things that will prove useful when it comes to implementing change. They may prove to make the difference between new methods failing or succeeding.

Move Towards Every-member Ministry

If the teaching of the New Testament is to be taken seriously, then we must recognise that every person within a church has something to contribute to the life of the church (1 Cor.12:12-30). Not everyone in your church will be able to preach, come up with creative ideas or demonstrate leadership ability, but they will all have some gift to offer. Without doubt the greatest resource that any church has is its membership. The problem is that, in most churches, almost all of the work is being done by about twenty percent of the church while the rest of the available gift is left dormant. This is partly because in every church there are people who are simply not willing to pull their weight. But it might also be because the leadership in the church has not identified the gifts available or ensured that each person in the church has a role.

Jesus told Peter to feed his sheep (John 21:15-17). The analogy of sheep is a good one when it comes to church members because both need to be guided. It is the responsibility of the leaders in a church to guide members of a church into roles that they can fulfil. The more people that are involved in the methods that you have devised, the more likely those methods are to succeed.

Identify Key People

As well as promoting every-member involvement, it is also important to identify key people to spearhead the work. With the best will in the world, not every member of the church will be able to head up a particular work or provide the vision and driving force necessary to carry it through. Enthusiasm is great, but it does not achieve the same as ability. There needs to be a core of capable and enthusiastic people who can carry the burden of an activity and ensure that it is done well.

I believe one of the most important skills of leadership is to identify these key people and delegate enough responsibility to them so that they have a fulfilling and demanding brief. There is nothing as powerful as assembling the 'movers and shakers' in your congregation and unleashing them into a particular task. Provided they are spiritual people who have correct motives and are accountable to the leadership of the church, they will be a potent force. Ultimately it is these key people who will really make things happen as far as outreach is concerned. Mobilize them and the results will ultimately follow.

Break Stereotype

One of the traps that will ensnarl progress is a fear of setting a precedent. Often church members will say, 'We never did that before'. It is true that if you are developing new structures to accommodate your methods you will be doing things that you never did before. This is not a negative thing; it is positive provided that change leads to greater effectiveness. Change for change's sake is never a good idea, but change that makes a church more effective is.

Ensure that your thinking doesn't become calcified or dominated by stereotypes. The New Testament does have a few things to say about church structure, but not many. There is no one prescribed way of structuring church life and the early church encompassed great variety. Erickson comments that 'the only didactic passages on church government are Paul's enumerations of the basic qualifications for offices'[2]. Individual churches in the New Testament were free to structure themselves in a way that was relevant to their own situation, and so are we. Be willing to break the stereotypes and don't feel that you need to copy anyone else. Each church must do what is appropriate in its own situation.

Be Courageous

It is important in this whole process to be courageous. Have the courage to try something new and to stand by your decisions even if, initially, they are not universally popular. Very few things can be achieved in a church without courage.

---

2   Erickson, *Christian Theology*, p.1094

Evaluation

The final stage in the process of developing a strategy is to have a rigorous evaluation. However much thought you might have put into the preceding stages you will not necessarily get it right the first time round. We are all fallible and our communities change so very quickly that some of our methods are almost bound to fail or be less effective than you initially envisaged. This is not a problem if your process is flexible in the first place. If at first you don't succeed, then try and try again.

A good evaluation will depend on honest critical thinking. But it requires more than that. You need to be positive as well, and believe that the right solution will be found in time. The problem with trial and error is that people can easily become disillusioned. This must be guarded against, and it is at this stage that the true qualities of leadership shine through. Visionary leaders are able to absorb disappointment, remain enthusiastic and be willing to reinvent a method so that it will be more effective. This will demand perseverance and a willingness to keep thinking but, as the alternative is a lack of progress, it is certainly worthwhile.

As you evaluate the work that has been done, two things will help keep you on the right track. First, keep your original goals at the back of your mind. Sometimes in the process of developing a strategy, you can loose sight of your goals. A church can become so wrapped up in the minutiae of detail that its vision fades and the forest cannot be seen for the trees. The goals you have set will be the constraints that prevent any derailing. If you remind yourself of them continually, you may fail to reach them at any one point, but you will have been going in the right direction.

Second, you will need to learn from your ongoing work. Even if a method fails to deliver, all is not lost. Valuable lessons will have been learned which if utilised will enable your church to do a better job the next time around. An old expression states: 'History teaches us that history teaches us nothing at all'. There might be a grain of truth in this, but only because people are not willing to learn from their mistakes. If lessons are learned then, inevitably, you will be in a better position to deal with a similar situation in a better way.

Questions

1 Analyse the effectiveness of your church in reaching out to
  unchurched people.
2 What goals do you think should be set for your church and
  why?
3 How would you go about achieving each of the goals you
  have suggested?
4 Think of ways in which people in your church can be
  mobilised to reach out and evangelise their community.

10

Needed Answers for New Questions

Inevitably, as we move out into the market place to share the gospel with people, we will be confronted with a great deal of scepticism. I have rarely come across anyone who, at our first meeting, wanted to commit themselves to the Christian faith. More usually, I meet people who are confused and don't know what to believe. Unless we take the time to deal with the confusion and clear up questions that they have, we will make little progress.

When Peter wrote his first epistle, he commanded the believers to be prepared to give an answer for the hope they had (1 Pet.3:15). The word that Peter uses here is *apologia* which was a legal term used in courtrooms when an argument is given on behalf of a client[1]. What Peter is telling us is that we need as Christians to contend for the faith when we come up against competing worldviews. Apologetics is the weapon we use when dealing with the many questions that we will face. As people express their doubts, we need to be ready to answer them honestly, boldly and with humility.

As we do this, there are some issues that we need to be aware of. First, there may be times when we don't have an answer that will fully satisfy the person we are witnessing to. Some years ago I was doing a mission in Malta. The GLO team I was with was conducting an open-air meeting along the sea front. I noted a woman who seemed interested in what we were saying so I approached her to share the gospel. She confessed that she had attended church since childhood, but then lost interest and fell away. When I asked her why, she gave an answer that clearly

---

1   Michaels, *1 Peter* (WBC), p.188

was not the real reason for her decision to leave the church. Gently I asked further questions to find the real reason. She then told me about a tragedy that removed any belief she had in God. She had a daughter who died, at the age of three, of leukaemia. 'Why did God allow that?' she asked me. I suppose I could have said that it was all down to original sin, but such an answer would have come across as trite and unsatisfying. In the end, I just told her that I didn't know, but I assured her of God's love for her and stated that God knows what it is like to lose a child.

The reality is that, sometimes, we don't know the answer to questions. In such situations we should never pretend that we do. It is better to admit that we don't know the answer, than to give one that achieves nothing. Sometimes it is good to ask for some time to think about it, and then come back to the person. But never let your pride push you into giving an answer that is half-baked.

Another thing we need to be aware of is the fact that we can win an argument but not win the person. When we do contend for the faith, the objective is not to browbeat the enquirer into intellectual submission but to clear up any difficulties they might have that prevent them from believing in God. Answering their questions in an argumentative or belligerent way will only cause further problems and put up more barriers to faith.

A third issue that we need to be aware of is that our arguments will not always be neatly packaged and tied up. Christianity is not something that can be proved scientifically. You will never be able to totally convince a sceptic that it is idiotic and blind not to accept what you believe in. What we can do, however, is to show that a person does not have to commit intellectual suicide to become a Christian and that Christianity is a coherent faith that provides some answers to life's deepest questions.

Finally we need to be aware that we cannot make a person a Christian simply by providing them with good answers to their questions. When all is said and done it is the Holy Spirit who convicts and draws people to faith in God. But the Holy Spirit uses our arguments to show people that the Christian faith is tenable and then reveals to them that it is true.

There are, of course, many questions that people today are asking. Too many by far to be dealt with in any one book, let alone in one chapter. What I will do is to mention the kind of questions I most often come across and then give what I feel is the best kind of answer to those questions.

Why Should I Bother Believing in God?

For many people in our postmodern world the issue is not about whether God exists but whether he is relevant. The ambivalence that many people have towards both religion and God is profound. Many just don't care. As one person said to me, 'Stephen if you want to believe in God that's fine, but don't expect me to think about it. I just couldn't be bothered.' We can of course quote all kinds of verses about judgment and hell, but this is rarely effective. In many cases it is precisely the threats of eternal punishment that have turned them off Christianity in the first place.

I would generally counter this ambivalence by pointing out that life has no ultimate meaning or value without God and the possibility of immortality. If there is no possibility of immortality then mankind and the universe as a whole will just fizzle out and become nothing. Mankind is therefore nothing more than 'a doomed race in a dying universe'[2]. Questions then need to be asked. Was there any real point to mankind existing in the first place? Would it have made any difference if mankind had never existed? If, like the animals, we exist and then we die then in that sense 'our life is not qualitatively different from that of a dog'[3]. And if there is no God then a mere duration of existence would not make our life meaningful. To live forever with no possibility of ascending to a higher plane would be ultimately meaningless. There would be no point to it. Only the existence of God and the possibility of knowing him can bring meaning to life.

Life would also have no ultimate value if there was no immortality and no God. If there was no possibility of punishment for the wrongs committed in this life, then what motivation is there for doing good? Why should we refrain from hurting others, if there is no one to answer to in the next life and therefore no repercussion to be faced? In any case, if God does not exist how do we decide what is right and wrong? Crimes

2   Craig, *Apologetics: An Introduction*, p.41
3   Craig, *Apologetics: An Introduction*, p.44

like rape and murder cannot be condemned as being wrong. All that we can conclude is that some of us, as individuals, do not like these things to be done. But that is purely subjective opinion. Hitler could not be condemned for gassing six million Jews. We do not like what he did but that is merely our opinion. Without a God to judge between right and wrong and to be a yardstick against which all actions moral or otherwise can be judged, there is no way of saying what is right or wrong. Only God can impose values on life.

To sum up, there are two good reasons for not being ambivalent about the subject of belief in God. If there is no God then life is devoid of ultimate meaning and there can be no objective moral values. As human beings we are nothing more than slime that evolved by sheer accident with no reason or purpose to our existence. We are insignificant people living a meaningless existence. Though this might possibly be the case, it would be an unbearable existence once the consequences of the non-existence of God had sunk in. It would also make the world as a whole unbearable – and is doing so. As Ravi Zacharias commented when summing up the destructive force of atheism in society, 'The infrastructure of our society has become mindless and senseless because the foundation upon which we have built cannot support any other kind of structure'[4]. Mankind therefore desperately needs God for, without God, life is absurd. That being the case, ambivalence towards God is not an option.

But Does God Exist?

Once the necessity of God is emphasized, I often find people asking if God really exists. Occasionally it is because they are convinced atheists. However, in the vast majority of cases, it is just because they are not sure that someone as intangible and apparently remote as God does actually exist. This could be termed agnosticism. They are not convinced that there is no God, but are not sure that there is a God.

I generally answer this kind of question in three ways. First, I mention the fact that the origin of the universe requires some kind of explanation. Perhaps the major alternative explanation for the existence of the universe is the theory of evolution. But

---

4   Zacharias, *Can Man live without God?* p.63

evolution is just that – a theory. And furthermore it is a theory that I personally find unconvincing. Evolutionists can take you back in stages of evolutionary development to the primitive gases from which everything else is said to have evolved, but they cannot explain the origin of matter or life. In that sense they, too, are taking a step of faith as they hold to their theory. It is also a theory that is increasingly under siege and in need of re-evaluation[5].

How then can we explain the origin of the universe? In order for the universe to have come into existence, there must have been something that caused it to exist but which was not itself caused. To use an analogy, if you see a train carriage moving along, and then another and then another, it is logical to deduce that at the end of these carriages there is an engine which is pushing them but which is not itself being pushed. Go back far enough in time, and you must have something or someone who created the universe but who was not created. Or to put it another way, the universe must depend for its existence on something that is totally independent[6]. By definition this must be God.

A second line of reasoning that I use is to talk about the inherent design and orderliness that appears to be present in the universe. This kind of argumentation was used effectively some two hundred years ago by William Paley[7]. He used the analogy of a watch, something that is very much more simple than the universe. Paley reasoned that if he came across a watch lying on the ground and inspected it, his conclusion, even if he had never seen a watch before, would be that it was something designed by an intelligent being rather than something that just happened to be there. He would reach this conclusion because the watch had many gears and a spring that worked together to make the hands move in perfect coordination with each other. If we would logically conclude that something as simple as a watch was designed and therefore had to have a designer, then the universe that is infinitely more complex and demonstrates much more sophisticated coordination also has to have a designer.

To suggest that the universe just happened, or that complex organs like the human eye came together without any thought

5   Johnston, *Darwin on Trial*, p.62

6   Williams, *The Case for God*, p.172

7   Paley, *Natural Theology, The Existence of God* Ed. J. Hick, p.100

or intent, is to stretch the point well beyond credulity. As William Dembski stated, 'undirected natural causes can throw scrabble pieces on a board but cannot arrange the pieces to form meaningful words or sentences'[8].

A third line that I would choose is to talk about the innate sense of morality that human beings seem to possess. We do not just react instinctively to situations but have a sense of what is right, wrong and noble. If the average man in the street were to be asked to comment on the holocaust or the actions of the Yorkshire Ripper he would immediately say that these were very evil acts. He may not know the basis on which he makes these moral assertions, but he would instinctively know they were wrong. Again people do make great personal sacrifices for the benefit of others. This moral sense cannot be explained as mere environmental conditioning since it occurs in the lives of people from every culture and background, though not necessarily in a uniform way. Neither can noble thoughts and actions find their origin in random evolutionary processes. They can, however, be understood if God exists. For he as a moral being can create us with a sense of morality, and this is precisely what the Bible claims.

How Do We Know the Bible is True?

Even if the people we witness to accept that there is a God and that mankind needs God, this position is still a long way from accepting the truth about God that is presented in scripture. This brings us to the issue of how we know the Bible is true. For many people the Bible is just another religious book, no different from the Koran or the Bhagavada Gita. Why do we as Christians believe that the Bible is the word of God and why do we believe that the manuscripts that we have today are correct?

I would tend to approach this question in a number of ways. First, I would deal with the philosophical issue of what is true and what is not true. In our postmodern society there is no such thing as absolute truth. Everyone has their own truth and no one truth can claim supremacy over another. The problem arises, however, when two truth claims prove to be mutually contradictory. For example, some people might claim that Chris-

---

8   Dembski, *Mere Creation*, Ed. Dembski, p.15

tians, Muslims and Hindus all worship the same God. But when you look at how the respective scriptures of these world religions describe the nature and character of God, the various accounts contradict each other. For the Christian, God is a trinity, for the Muslim, god is one, and for the Hindu, there are many gods. Such contradictory views cannot all be right. To say otherwise is as illogical as suggesting that red and blue are actually the same colour. It may be politically correct, but it is foolish, and insufficient evidence to risk anything as serious as our eternal destiny.

The next step would be to show positively why the Bible is both the word of God and a document that has been handed down to us in a reliable form. We do this by first mentioning that the Bible itself claims to be the word of God. This in itself is not proof, but it is the obvious starting point. Next we mention that, although the Bible was written by more than forty authors from vastly different backgrounds and cultural perspectives, and although this writing took place over a period of 1200 years, there still remains a single thread throughout and that thread is God's plan of salvation for humanity.

In addition to this remarkable fact, we need to focus on the prophecies in scripture that came true and thus add considerable weight to belief in the inspired nature of the Bible. Indeed scripture itself makes it clear that fulfilled prophecy is evidence of the divine origin of the prophecy (Jer.28:9 ; Deut.18:21-22). In the Old Testament there are three kinds of prophecy[9]. First there are predictions about the coming of the Messiah. Second there are predictions about kings, nations and cities. Third, there are predictions about the Jews. These predictions are not vague but very specific, even to the point of naming people, places and specific actions. In particular, the prophecies that are linked with the birth, life and death of Jesus Christ are so specific, even though some of them were given nearly a thousand years before the time of Christ, that they could not possibly be taken as coincidental.

Perhaps the most powerful argument in favour of the Bible being the word of God is the testimony of Jesus on the matter. Jesus unequivocally put his full seal of approval on the Old Testament (Matt.5:18) and he continually quoted the Old Testa-

---

9   Little, *Know Why You Believe*, pp.68-69

ment, applying it to situations that he found himself in. He also stated that his followers would receive divine help so that they could pass on what they saw and heard for successive generations. The recommendations of Jesus as well as the comments made by the New Testament writers clearly demonstrate the divine nature of the New Testament. If Jesus is God, and there is ample evidence to substantiate that claim, and if he declared the Bible to be the word of God, then it must be accepted as such.

There remains one last strand to the argument. How do we know that the biblical text we have in our hands has the same content as the document that was originally penned? After all, none of the original documents exists today. This is a huge and complex issue, but we have nevertheless good reason for accepting that the documents we have are a reliable record.

When it comes to the Old Testament, we can have a sense of confidence because of the detailed copying methods that the ancient scribes used. The basis for the present text of the Hebrew Bible is the Masoretic text and this is the prototype against which all other texts are compared[10]. The Masoretes gave painstaking detail to their work of copying the text. As they worked on a scroll they ensured that each page on the scroll was copied exactly, line for line and word for word[11]. They checked and cross-checked each sheet before it was sewn to the rest of the scroll. When a book was completed they subjected it to more checks including how many times each letter of the alphabet occurred in the scroll. Such fine attention to detail results in a very high degree of accuracy in the copying technique. The discovery of the Dead Sea Scrolls has also provided considerable confirmation of the integrity of the copying as they give comparative texts that are a thousand years older than the Masoretic texts.

We can have confidence in the integrity of the New Testament documents because of the sheer number of manuscripts that we have available to us. There are some 13,000 manuscript copies of whole books or portions that can be compared to each other.[12]

---

10   Norton, 'Texts and Manuscripts of the Old Testament', *The Origin of the Bible*, Ed. Philip Comfort, p.154

11   Scrolls were made from sheets of papyrus or leather that were then sewn together to make one long sheet that could be rolled up into a scroll.

12   Copley, *About the Bible*, p.78

This is a far greater number of texts than for any other ancient document. As different manuscripts from distant places are brought together, the level of their similarity is evidence of how far back in time the documents from which these manuscripts were copied are placed. This gives a very clear picture of just how reliable the copies that we possess really are. The embarrassment of wealth in the textual tradition can give us complete confidence in the integrity of the present New Testament text.

Why is Christianity the Only Way?

I often find that, when I am making headway contending for the truthfulness of Christianity, people respond by accepting that the Christian faith is true, but insist that it is not the only truth. In our postmodern society not only is everyone's holy scripture valid, but everyone's faith is true for the practitioner. We all have our own way of getting to God, but we all get there in the end and no one can say that their route is the best. It is merely the best for them. This tolerance of diversity is the very essence of postmodernity.

This kind of question is difficult to answer for at least three reasons. First, to contend with a question like this is to attack the very heart of our pluralist society and therefore Christians who hold to the uniqueness of Christianity are castigated as intolerant bigots. Second, many people who hold to a pluralist world view are not so much concerned with fact and evidence as with political correctness and the acceptance of others. Third, we are dealing with a profoundly emotional issue, for to say that some faiths are wrong is to say that many sincere and devout Muslims and Hindus are going to a lost eternity. This is of course the truth, but it is a doctrine that is unpalatable to most contemporary people.

I would begin dealing with this issue in the same way that I deal with questions about the divine nature of scripture. When all is said and done, two contradictory ideas cannot both be true. Logically if they are different, then one must be right and one must be wrong. However unpalatable this may seem in our tolerant society, it simply does not make sense to argue otherwise. I would also point out that most other world religions would also claim that they are true. As Ravi Zacharias notes, 'at the very heart of every religion is an uncompromising commitment to a particular way of defining who God is or is not and accordingly, of defining life's purpose'[13]. The Christian is therefore not alone in claiming the uniqueness of his faith.

At this point I would state that the thing that makes Christianity unique among all the religions of the world is the person of Jesus Christ. Christianity is unique because Jesus is unique. This then focuses the sceptic's mind firmly on the person of Christ, and that is where the focus should remain. The validity of the Christian faith is based on the person of Christ and what he did. If Christ can be seen to be unique, then the uniqueness of Christianity will be self evident. But in what ways is Christ unique?

First, Jesus is unique because he came into the world without a human father being involved in his conception. He, unlike any other man who has ever lived, was born of a virgin. The issue of the virgin birth is of course doubted by many, but such doubts cannot be sustained. Mary and Joseph could have gained nothing from the claim that the baby Jesus was not actually Joseph's son. The scandal would have been painful for them to bear, and not one they would have willingly endured, were it not for the fact that Jesus was conceived as a result of the activity of the Holy Spirit. Zacharias and Elizabeth would equally have nothing to gain by allowing their son, John the Baptist, to play second fiddle to his younger cousin Jesus, especially in a society where the pecking order within family life was so important. They willingly allowed John to play this role, and even die by the sword, because they knew the miraculous way in which Jesus came into the world. Anyone who attempts to deny the virgin birth must also explain the behaviour of these two couples, but no credible explanation can be found. That makes Jesus unique, for Mohammed, Krishna and Buddha all came into the world as a result of a conventional and ordinary birth.

Second, Jesus is unique for his life was one of utter moral purity. His adversaries continually tried to trip him up and find some way of accusing him, but their efforts were in vain. Jesus himself challenged his opponents to accuse him of sin but they could not. At his trial, as false witnesses told all kinds of lies about him, the judge stated that no fault could be found in him. By their own admission, this could not be said of

---

13 Zacharias, *Jesus among other Gods*, p.7

Mohammed, Buddha or Krishna[14]. Their struggles are recorded within the pages of their own scriptures. In Surahs 47 and 48 Mohammed was told to ask for forgiveness for sin[15]. The Bhagavad Gita describes the exploits of Krishna with the milk-maids. As for the Buddha, the very fact that he had to endure the many rebirths of reincarnation points to many imperfect lives. In each case their lives were less than completely holy, but Jesus led a life of purity that no one could question.

Third, Jesus is unique because he performed many miracles that can be historically attested. Again there are those who doubt the miracles of Christ. These doubts can be dealt with by pointing out the reasonableness of the belief in Christ's miracles. The miracles of Jesus were done in a public setting for all to see. This meant that, among those who witnessed these miracles, were opponents of Jesus who clearly would not want to accept their validity because genuine miracles would in themselves validate Christ's claim to have come from God. Furthermore, Jesus' miracles varied from control over nature to the healing of diseases and even bringing people back from the dead. They were performed over a period of three years and in environments that could not be controlled in the way that magicians control their stage show. Some of Jesus' miracles were openly attested after the event. The healings, for example, were proved to be valid by those who had been healed. It would be hard to convince Lazarus after his resurrection that the miracle that brought him back to life was bogus.

Some sceptics might still argue that those who witnessed Jesus' miracles were primitive people who could easily be hood-winked by clever conjuring tricks. Even if this were true, it would be hard to see how a carpenter from Nazareth could perform elaborate conjuring tricks on the scale of the feeding of the five thousand, and get away with it. After all, no one actually denied that something marvellous had happened when Jesus performed his miracles. The fact is, however, that those people who saw Jesus performing miracles were not gullible fools. I have already mentioned that many of the people who witnessed the miracles of Jesus were enemies who would desperately want to prove that all he did was nothing more than a hoax. If their

---

14   Zacharias, *Jesus among other Gods*, p.40
15   *Koran*, Surahs 47 & 48, pp.359-360

objections could be voiced then Jesus would no longer be a threat to them. They therefore watched the miracles, not with open minds ready to accept and believe, but with bitter cynicism, desperately hoping to humiliate Jesus and show him to be a fraud. But despite their vehement opposition to Jesus they simply could not show his miracles to be false. We have no record, either in the Bible or outside of it, that casts any doubt on the reality of the miracles. It is more logical, therefore, to believe that they did indeed happen – and this makes Jesus unique.

Fourth, Jesus is unique because he actually claimed to be God. He did so in several ways. He used the term 'Abba' when addressing God in prayer. This was a term of familiarity rather akin to the modern 'daddy' which no Jew would have dared to use. He claimed that he was the only person who could reveal the Father to men (Matt.11:27) and that he himself was the absolute revelation of God (John 14:9). He claimed to have power over demonic forces (Luke 11:20), to be able to perform miracles (Matt.11:4,5) and to forgive sin (Luke 5:20). Jesus also claimed that he controlled the eternal destiny of men (Luke 12:8,9). All these things could only be done by God, and in claiming them, this is exactly what Jesus was saying about himself. This not only makes Jesus unique, it also forces us to decide what kind of being he was. As C. S. Lewis stated, when you think of the enormity of Jesus' claims, he was either 'a megalomaniac compared with whom Hitler was the most sane and humble of men' or 'a complete lunatic suffering from that form of delusion which undermines the whole mind of man', or he was indeed God[16].

Fifth, Jesus is unique because he rose from the dead. The resurrection is undoubtedly the greatest miracle associated with the life of Christ. It was one that is remarkable not least for the fact that Jesus himself predicted the resurrection long before it ever happened (Matt. 16:21). The evidence for the resurrection of Christ is based on four facts, all of which can be historically attested. These are that he was dead; that he was buried; that the tomb in which he was buried was subsequently found to be empty; and Christ's post-mortem appearances to his followers and to others.

16   Lewis, *God in the Dock*, p.81

The fact of his death is not difficult to establish. Bearing in mind the flogging he received and the agonies of crucifixion, the suggestion that he merely fainted and later recovered in the cool of the tomb is absurd. In any case, his executioners were professionals who did not make mistakes. When executioners got bored waiting for their victims to die, they broke their legs so that asphyxiation and a swift death would follow. When they came to Jesus these experienced executioners did not bother to break his legs because they knew him to be dead already. What is more, a spear had been thrust into the side of Jesus and the gospel records state that blood and water flowed out (John 19:34). Though the gospel writers could not have been aware of the significance of this, it strongly suggests that Jesus died of heart failure.

The fact of his burial is equally easy to verify. We are told that Jesus was buried in the tomb of Joseph of Arimathea. Joseph was a wealthy and prominent man and a member of the Sanhedrin, the Jewish parliament. There is no way that a prominent figure like Joseph could have his name linked with the scandal of Jesus and his death as a criminal if it were not true. Members of the Sanhedrin were simply too well known to allow false stories to be linked to them without the stories being exposed as false[17].

Then there are the accounts of the empty tomb. These too can be verified. If a sceptic were to deny the resurrection, he would have to come up with an alternative suggestion as to why the tomb was empty. Given that the Roman guard was stationed around the tomb, the thought of the disciples stealing the body is simply preposterous[18]. The only other people likely to remove the body were the Jewish or Roman authorities, but neither would have anything to gain from doing so. What is more, at Pentecost, the disciples were preaching about the resurrection of Jesus in the very same city where he was crucified and buried. The Jewish leaders would have loved to silence the disciples, as their impact among the Jewish populace was enormous. The Romans, too, would have been uncomfortable about the stir that this kind of preaching was causing. Both parties could have destroyed Christianity forever, even before it began, simply by

---

17   Lewis, *God in the Dock*, p.186
18   McDowell, *The Resurrection Factor*, pp.56-60

producing the body of Jesus. They could not do this because they did not have the body. Given the lack of alternative explanations for the empty tomb, the only acceptable one is that Jesus did indeed rise from the dead.

Finally there are the post-mortem appearances of Jesus. He appeared to individuals, to small groups and to 500 people at once. The range of appearances, and the fact that Jesus talked to people and ate with them rules out the possibility of these appearances being hallucinations. There is also compelling evidence from the testimony of Paul who opposed the church but then dramatically changed the whole course of his life, spending his remaining years propagating the gospel. Such a turn-around can only be explained by a resurrection appearance. James, too, was a sceptic even though he was a brother of Jesus. He, too, changes his mind, becomes a leader of the church and, according to Josephus, died for his faith in Christ[19]. His dramatic reversal can only be explained if you accept that he saw the risen Christ and was convinced. All this evidence leads to only one conclusion, that Jesus died and was raised from the dead. His return from death undoubtedly makes him unique and this in turn makes Christianity unique.

The Role of the Holy Spirit in Evangelism

Even when all of this evidence has been presented and all the questions that have been thrown at us have been answered, that in itself is still not enough to bring people to faith in Christ. A good apologist can present a compelling argument in favour of the Christian faith, but he cannot convict a person of sin. This is the work of the Holy Spirit. That being the case, as well as being prepared to answer the many doubts that our postmodern generation will throw up, we need to be prayerful, asking God to break through the scepticism of the age and penetrate into people's hearts. Only this will bring about genuine conversions.

Questions

1 Which of the questions asked in this chapter do you think are the most pertinent and why?

---

19 Josephus, *The Complete Works*, p.428

2 What other questions have you come across in your
   evangelism and how did you answer them?
3 How do we get the balance between presenting reasoned
   arguments in our evangelism, and relying on the convicting
   work of the Holy Spirit?

11

Life in a Strange World

If we do think about our evangelistic methods and mobilise the church to witness, then, God willing, we will see people come to faith in Jesus Christ. But what next? My wife and I were shocked some time ago with a news item of a little baby girl who was abandoned by her mother in a small lane on the verge of a large housing estate. The situation was desperate since the child was so young and vulnerable. Any baby left like that would die if not found quickly.

The Bible describes new Christians as babies. They, too, are spiritually vulnerable and need constant care and supervision in the first few weeks and months of their spiritual lives. This will have a number of implications for those who have been witnessing to them and have brought them to a point of commitment. If new Christians are spiritual babies, then the Christians who witnessed to them are the spiritual parents. What is their role in relation to these new Christians?

When writing to the Thessalonian believers, Paul told this infant church that when he first brought them the gospel, his love for them was such that he and his companions also shared with them their very lives (1 Thess.2:8). As their spiritual father he committed himself to these Christians rather than remaining aloof and detached as they came to terms with their new found faith[1]. This is precisely what we must learn to do with new Christians. They need commitment and support from more mature Christians which will require not only time being spent with them, but constant prayers for them (1 Thess. 1:2). A quick glance at any of Paul's epistles will reveal the extent of his knowledge of and interest in the affairs of those he influenced

---

1   Wanamaker, *The Epistle to the Thessalonians*, p.102

for Christ. If this care is not mirrored in our treatment of new Christians, there will be many casualties along the way.

Is This the Church or Mars?

New Christians need more than nurturing and someone to role model the Christian life for them; they also need to be brought gently into the life of the church. Every year we take our college students to a large mosque in the heart of Glasgow. We do this so that the students, who are training to serve God, can gain an understanding of Islam and meet some Muslim devotees first hand.

I have always found it fascinating to monitor the students as they enter this very different environment. The truth is that they rarely feel comfortable. Most of them have never been to a mosque before, though they have heard a lot about mosques. What they have been told by others is not always accurate. When they get there they quickly realise that they know no one and feel keenly that they are just visitors. Most of the worshippers have a different style of dress to my students. It is an environment full of strange sounds and smells. A place where everyone else seems to know what they are doing. There are a lot of unspoken rules which strangers will not understand and events which mystify the uninitiated. All of this makes the students feel profoundly uncomfortable and confused. This is exactly how a new Christian feels when he goes for the first time to a church.

Church really is a strange place to be if you are unaccustomed to it. Those of us who come from Christian families are not always aware of just how strange a place church is. This is because we grew up with it and feel automatically at home. But for someone who has not been used to going to church, it is a bit like a foreign land.

To begin with, people in society at large rarely sing together. But church is full of singing, both contemporary songs and ancient hymns. Most people are not used to sitting down for a protracted period of time and listening to a monologue. In most churches, however, sermons are preached weekly. Most people only dress up if they are going to a party or perhaps to their office job. Many churches, on the other hand, have dress codes which the bulk of the congregation will adhere to. Most people

have only a few close friends, but there are a great many churches, even large ones, where there is a real sense of unity, friendship and camaraderie.

Unwritten Laws

This, however, is just the beginning. Every church will have its
own unwritten laws and secret language. Recently I was invited
to preach at a church in Denmark. Before I spoke we celebrated
communion, something I do in my home church every week.
The difference was that in this church they used lots of tiny cups
for the communion wine rather than the one shared cup that we
have in my church. I was not put off by this because I have often
gone to churches where individual cups were used. The deacon
serving the wine approached me first because I was sitting in
the front row. I took my little cup and closed my eyes prayerfully. In other churches that I had gone to where individual cups
were used, all the communicants hold their cup until the chair-
man gives the signal, and they all drink their wine together. In
this church things were slightly different. The custom was to
drink your wine immediately and give the cup back to the deacon who is distributing them. I heard a forced cough and looked
up only to see the deacon still standing in front of me waiting
for me to get on with it. Embarrassed, I obliged, but no one had
told me that this is how it was done in that particular church.

On another occasion I invited an Anglican friend of mine to
share communion in a church that I used to attend. She was
used to having a minister conduct the service from the front. I
come from a Brethren church where lay participation is much
more common. In this particular church musical instruments
were not used in communion services. Instead there had been a
member of the church deputed to sound the first note of the
hymn in a booming voice, and then the rest of us would join in.
It so happened that the song leader was sitting directly behind
us. A member of the church asked for a particular hymn to be
sung. For my friend this was strange because she had never
experienced this kind of open worship before. Once everyone
had found the place in their hymn books they all stood up. This
again was strange to my friend because no one had told us to
stand, it was just assumed by everyone because this is what was
generally done. Suddenly the song leader began with such vol-

ume that it could have been mistaken for a sonic boom. I smiled as my friend jumped with fright, but then realised just how difficult the whole experience was proving to be for her.

These are just two of the many examples that illustrate the point. If established Christians find it strange going to churches that they do not usually frequent; if they struggle to understand all the unwritten laws and to interpret the unique language and terminology of a different church, how much more difficult will an unchurched person find it.

There is a sense in which we will never be able to get rid of the customs and idiosyncrasies of church life. Indeed it would be wrong to do so, because every church must have some structure and a certain individuality. The church will ultimately reflect the people who comprise it and, just as each individual has his or her own idiosyncrasies and taste, so their church consists in some measure of an accumulation of idiosyncrasies. However, there are a couple of things that we need to do when new converts come along to our churches. First, we need to explain what will happen in any given church service so that there will be the minimum of bemusement. This is a simple thing, but it can make the difference between a person feeling uncomfortable and out of place and feeling that it was an interesting as well as a positive experience. In my own church, whenever someone comes for the first time, one of the leaders of the church will welcome them and take a few minutes to explain what will go on in the programme, and why. This simple courtesy has the effect of putting our visitors at ease.

A second thing we must do is to ensure that what we do in church is thoroughly biblical. Of course there will be many traditions in every church that never get a mention in the Bible. Many churches, for example, delegate someone to stand at the front door to welcome everyone as they come in. You never read about this practice in the Bible, though I think it is a good one. Almost all churches use hymn books or overhead projectors, and obviously these were never available in New Testament times. These traditions are actually helpful and logical. However, some churches insist on traditions that are neither logical nor helpful. These have no biblical justification. Sooner or later, new converts will ask the question why? If there is no biblical justification for these things, then why do we do them? Too many of these meaningless traditions will lead to frustration and confusion.

One example that comes to mind is the times of church services. Some years ago I was in a church that conducted an evangelistic service every Sunday at 7.00 pm. This proved to be a bad time because most families were putting their children to bed at this time. It was unlikely, therefore, that any non-Christians would ever come to this service. It was suggested that the service be switched to the morning to make it easier for people to attend. This inevitably meant that the communion service had to be shifted to the evening slot. Unfortunately there was great resistance to this move, despite the fact that it was so logical. The reason for the opposition was not because of biblical principles – frankly there were none – it was just that things had always been done this way and the tradition took precedence over commonsense and scripture. For those who had always grown up in the church this did not seem ridiculous, but for those church members who were new to the place the whole issue was utterly absurd. No wonder! Such unbiblical traditions make no sense at all. It was inevitable that this conflict would discourage many of the new Christians and make them feel that the Bible was not as valued as it should be. This unfortunate situation needs to be avoided at all cost, as it will inevitably lead to disillusionment and will hamper growth both in the lives of individuals and in the church as a whole.

Another aspect of church life that we need to explain to new Christians is what the church does. Not only do new Christians struggle to understand all the traditions of church life, they also take a while to fully comprehend what church is all about. The importance of what the church does needs to be spelt out and new converts need help to appreciate the significance of the church's role.

Teaching

Although the church does many things, there are four functions of church life that need to be identified and explained. These are teaching, fellowship, worship and witness. The need for teaching within the church is self-evident. Christianity is an intelligent faith that is based on truths, communicated to us through the Bible. However unfashionable sermons may be there is no getting away from the fact that God's word does need to be taught if the church is to learn how to live and serve God. For

new Christians, however, the average sermon will often be a little above their heads. This cannot be avoided because the rest of
the church needs to be spiritually fed. If some of the new Christians were not accustomed to going to church before their conversion, the very act of sitting and listening to a half-hour sermon might in itself be daunting. They will need to be primed
and prepared for this.

There are a few steps that we can teach them in order to help
them get the most out of the sermon[2]. For example, they can
pray before the service and ask God to help them understand
what is being said. They can also read the scripture passage
beforehand and then note how the preacher unpacks it. Keeping
the Bible open during the sermon so as to follow the logic of the
passage is also helpful. If they are encouraged to take notes during the sermon they can review them afterwards. They can also
be encouraged to note down every question that arises in their
minds as the preacher is speaking. These can be put to the
preacher at the end of the service and this will prove helpful to
preacher and listener alike. It is also very useful if there is the
opportunity after the sermon for church members to discuss the
sermon informally. In our church we have coffee at the end of
the service and this enables us to ask each other what we
learned and found helpful in the sermon.

Even when you encourage the new Christians in this way,
they will still need teaching appropriate to their level. My personal feeling is that a one-to-one discipleship course is the ideal.
There are three reasons for this. First, it demonstrates to the new
Christians that they are valued and it is worth investing time
solely in them. Second, their personal spiritual needs are catered
for and their questions are dealt with. Third, the person doing
the discipleship course with them will be a spiritual mentor and
will be ideally placed to role model a Christian lifestyle.

The key factor in this discipleship course will be to teach
material that is appropriate to the needs of the new Christian.
For example, it will be entirely inappropriate to teach new converts about prophecy or the theological themes in the book of
Leviticus because they are simply not at that stage. On the other
hand, it will be appropriate to teach them about the Christian
lifestyle, prayer, the assurance of salvation and the work of the

---

2   See McQuoid, *Guide to God's Family*, pp.38-41

Holy Spirit. These basics are what they need to grasp quickly so that they can begin to grow. One of my friends pointed out to me that in India, where he is a missionary, they begin by teaching new converts about the life and teachings of Christ. Passages like the Sermon on the Mount have a great deal to say about the basic issues of Christian living. Such a teaching programme also fits into the command that Jesus himself gave in his Great Commission, that we should teach everything that he taught (Matt 28:20). This seems eminently sensible.

As well as teaching new Christians we need to encourage them to read the Bible for themselves. There are also many Bible reading plans and devotional notes that will prove to be useful. I also think it is valuable to encourage new Christians to get into the habit of reading through the whole Bible. With 1189 chapters the Bible will seem an impossibly daunting book, but there are some Bible reading plans that take the reader through the Bible by picking out just a few key chapters here and there. This will enable the same objective to be reached within a less daunting framework[3].

Worship

Another important function of the church is that of worship. Here, too, a different world opens up to new Christians. For those of us who have grown up in the church or who have been Christians for a long time, worship is a wonderful experience. Our knowledge of God fills us with a sense of awe that compels us to worship. We understand the worship traditions of our own church and can easily fit into the mindset of structured worship. We have also learned to appreciate the particular form of worship that is carried out in our local church. For a new Christian, however, especially one with no experience of church life, it can be a daunting and even confusing experience.

New Christians certainly understand that Christ died for them and has saved them, but they will probably not appreciate the sheer greatness of God. The attributes of omnipresence, omniscience and omnipotence will be a mystery to them. Their knowledge and appreciation of these things will require time to grow. When it does, their sense of wonder and desire for wor-

---

3   See McQuoid, *A New Kind of Living*, pp.169-175

ship will also grow, but this takes time. They will also be unfamiliar with the worship experience and format of their new church.

I grew up within a Christian Brethren tradition where members of the congregation participate in public worship. In a typical worship service someone opens the service by reading a passage of scripture that sets the theme for the service. Those participants who are familiar with the format then make their contribution to the worship service and generally keep to the theme set by the person who opened the service. Of course no official rule stated that participants follow this theme, but it is a tradition that developed over many years of church practice. On one occasion a Christian friend who was not familiar with this tradition came to our church and participated in the service by asking for a hymn to be sung and then praying. What he said in his prayer was very real and helpful, as was the hymn which he requested, but it did not fit in with the overall theme of the service. This was not his fault, for he did not understand the unwritten rules of that type of worship. Some of the older members of the congregation, though very appreciative of his contribution, nevertheless put the whole experience down to his spiritual immaturity. Not so! He was just not used to the particular ethos of worship. A new Christian who has never been to church before will be in exactly the same position.

When it comes to acclimatising new Christians to the concept of worship there are a number of things we need to stress. First, it is important that they know that a life committed to God is an act of worship in itself. Indeed what we did during a worship service would be irrelevant – and indeed unacceptable to God – if the life we lived outside of church was a denial of Christ. Worship is therefore something we do every day.

Second, our worship needs to be sincere. However much or little we understand about God and his will, he knows us intimately and can read our very thoughts. Those of us who have been Christians for years know how easy it is to become complacent in our worship. If we are not careful it is all too easy to slip into a habit of singing songs that we do not think about, or to say 'Amen' at the end of a prayer that we have not even listened to. It is the act of engaging our minds and hearts and expressing our profound gratitude to God that is at the very heart of worship. This needs to be done with utter sincerity.

New Christians need to know that even the most bumbling utterances of thanks, offered sincerely from a pure heart, are more important than the most polished phrases or theologically correct expressions.

Third, we need to communicate to new Christians that worship is an intelligent exercise. Worship should never be cold and purely rational, but if we are to express our appreciation of the greatness of God, we need to know who he really is. In that sense, worship is closely related to theology. Without an understanding of God, our worship can become a repetitive series of bland platitudes that say nothing about the God we claim to adore. But once we grasp something of the wonder of God, our worship will become enlivened and intelligent. When we run discipleship classes for new Christians, we must take this into consideration.

Fourth, we need to communicate that true worship involves emotion. God has given us feelings and these are to be used appropriately within the context of worship. These feelings will enable us to get excited about God and express our appreciation of him enthusiastically. Though we need to teach new Christians to express their emotions appropriately, they also need to realise that they should not be afraid of their emotions as they are a natural vehicle for expressing how we feel. If there is no sense of awe as we approach our majestic God, and no sense of wonderment and excitement when we think of all that he has done for us, then there is something profoundly wrong with our spiritual walk.

Prayer

Another area where orientation will be necessary is that of prayer. Again, for people who have been Christians for a long time, prayer is something that comes naturally and easily. But, for a new Christian, prayer can be an extremely difficult thing. However, as prayer is at the very heart of the Christian life, this is an area to which much attention must be focused.

Emphasising the beauty of prayer is where this orientation must begin. By prayer we enter the immediate presence of God without the need of any intermediaries. The moment we pray God hears every word and begins responding to our plans. This fellowship with our Father is essential for spiritual health and it is for this reason that the Bible encourages us to pray continually (1 Thess.5:17). This knowledge, in itself, does not make prayer any easier, but an awareness of the necessity of prayer will encourage new Christians to work hard at it.

I have often found that it is necessary to pray with new Christians so they can hear for themselves how natural it is. It has also been helpful to encourage them to relax and be themselves in prayer. Since the use of formal words is unnecessary, they should be encouraged to express what they feel in prayer and as the habit grows, words will come more readily.

I would like to suggest some guidelines, which could give new Christians some structure to their prayer lives.

1. Discipline yourself to spend at least 20 minutes each day reading your Bible and praying. Ensure that this is a priority!
2. Find somewhere quiet where you can pray without interruptions or distractions.
3. Begin your prayer time by thanking God for all he has been doing in your life and worship him for who he is.
4. You may find it helpful to pray out loud. This will help you concentrate and think about what you are saying.
5. Keep a prayer diary so that you can list the kind of things you should be praying about and then cross off the list any prayers that have been answered. This will help you pray consistently and encourage you as you see prayers answered.

These points are very simple and routine, but they are helpful ways of encouraging new Christians to pray during the early months of their Christian life.

Witness

A fourth area where new Christians need help is when it comes to witnessing to others. As they begin in their new found faith they will discover that people will relate to them in different ways. Some of their friends will snigger and think the whole thing is a little silly. Others will oppose and openly criticise them. Still others will be ambivalent and in some cases be very pleased for them. It will be important to prepare them for every possible reaction and to encourage them to talk openly to their friends about the decision they have made. Once the news of their new found faith is out in the open they will be vulnerable to the opinions of their friends, but they will have made their first stand as Christians.

New Christians need to do more than just be open about their faith. They need to learn to share it with others. This can be very daunting indeed and they will need your support as they take their first few steps as witnesses for Jesus Christ. There are, of course, many examples of people who become Christians and are so fired up and enthusiastic about their faith that they need no encouragement to witness. They do so boldly and seem to want to tell the whole world that they have trusted in Jesus Christ. When this is the case it is wonderful, but even then they need some input so that when they witness they will do so tactfully and with grace and wisdom.

I remember some years ago while working in the Republic of Ireland, coming across a young Christian from a small country town near where I was staying. He had been a Christian for only a couple of years, and, though an enthusiastic evangelist, he was already running into serious trouble. The town in which he grew up was almost entirely Roman Catholic, and a very conservative brand of Catholicism was practised. Once this young man became a Christian, he grew very angry that in all his years of faithfully attending the Roman Catholic Church he had never heard a clear presentation of the gospel. He was determined to share the good news with every person in the town so they, too, could find true faith. His motives were pure and his enthusiasm commendable. His methodology, however, left much to be desired. He wrote to publishers in the USA looking for tracts that would be 'anti-Catholic'. When he found one, he bought 10,000 copies and distributed them to every house in the district. The particular tract he used was very offensive, and the whole population was outraged to the point where he had become an outcast. This problem could have been avoided had he been given some guidance as a young Christian about how to witness.

One of the important things to bear in mind when working with young Christians is that they have all the contacts. Inevitably, the longer a person goes to church and gets involved in the life of the church, the more Christians he will befriend. Conversely this will almost always mean that he will have fewer close friends who are non-Christians. As I mentioned earlier in this book, when I deliver my evangelism lectures at Tilsley College, I ask my students to make a list of their ten closest friends. Then I ask them to put a mark next to the ones who are Christians. In most cases the vast majority of their close friends will be Christians. In some cases it is also possible to see a fairly strong link between the length of time a person has been involved in church life and the number of close friends he has who are non-Christians.

When a person first becomes a Christian, in all probability most of his closest friends will not be Christians. This can be a pressure, and the church needs to learn to support the new Christian for this reason. However, it is also a great opportunity to reach his peer group with the gospel. This will involve his living a consistent Christian life in front of them and tactfully sharing what Christ means to him, especially when questions are raised. In order for both of these things to be achieved, the church will actively need to provide advice and support.

Questions

1 What aspects of your church life do you think would seem strange to someone who was unchurched?
2 In a typical service, what would have to be explained to an outsider if they were to appreciate what was going on?
3 Four functions of church life are mentioned in this chapter. They are: teaching, worship, prayer and witnessing. What does your church do to encourage new Christians to get involved in these activities?
4 What practical steps could your church take to ensure that new Christians feel part of your church community?

12

The Baggage Handlers

I have decided that flying anywhere is terribly inconvenient. The problem is not the travel itself, it is all the packing that has to be done. I hate packing and am pretty useless at it. Invariably I leave behind the most important things. Since getting married I have wisely left this side of things to my wife. She never forgets anything and for that I am very thankful. The problem is that she has such a knack of including everything but the kitchen sink. Any time we travel the suitcases seemed to weigh about half a ton! A simple long weekend will produce a big enough collection of baggage to elongate my arms several centimetres as I carry it out to the car.

As a result I have developed a sympathy for baggage handlers at the airport. While it is true that they have little respect for people's property, often treating the baggage contemptuously, they still have a hard job taking my enormous and weighty suitcases and putting them into the hold of the aircraft. These men and women are not the only kind of baggage handlers and this packaging is not the only baggage.

When it comes to church life there are plenty of people who carry baggage around with them. Many people have skeletons in the cupboard and issues that spill over from their past life. This can be seen with new Christians who make a commitment to Christ and then have to deal with many issues that will hamper their Christian life. The church cannot ignore this baggage. It can be very weighty, and for this reason churches often treat it with the same rough contempt that airport handlers treat their baggage. Whether we like it or not, however, the baggage is there and needs to be dealt with. If we, as churches, are serious about evangelism at all, then we need to learn to be good baggage handlers.

Moral Baggage

There are two main types of baggage that need to be dealt with. First, there is moral baggage and, second, there is emotional baggage. Moral baggage is those issues that affect a person's life because of sin. Much of this baggage, of course, would not be perceived by our relativistic society as a problem. We live in a society where the use of recreational drugs, drunkenness, homosexuality and pre-marital sex are considered to be the norm rather than things that are morally questionable. Indeed in our postmodern world the word morality is going out of fashion. People do not do wrong things, they do not sin, they merely make lifestyle choices. What one person decides is right, another might object to, but this is a personal choice as opposed to a moral issue.

We, as Christians, have a very different way of looking at morality. We believe in an objective set of values, based on the character of God and revealed to us in scripture. The problem is that, as unchurched people become Christians, they may be completely unaware of these values and may already be involved in a lifestyle that is a far cry from a biblical one. Some of these lifestyle issues may be ingrained and highly complex.

The question may well be asked, did these new Christians not repent of their sin when they became Christians? This is frankly a simplistic way of looking at the issue. First, they may not have been aware at the time of their conversion that some of their actions were sinful. One friend of mine became a Christian because he knew that his attitudes and actions fell short of God's standards. He knew what sin was and knew that some of the things he said, did and thought were sinful. He repented and became a Christian. At the time he was also living with his girlfriend and they were not married. When he became a Christian he genuinely had no idea that this kind of a relationship was sinful. In his culture, as in much of the West, marriage was the exception rather than the norm. His problem was not that he was rebelling deliberately against the will of God. Quite the reverse. He was repenting because he wanted to follow God. However, he had no idea that cohabiting with his girlfriend was a sin. For this reason he could genuinely be repentant, determined to follow God and a committed Christian, even though he was still 'living in sin'.

This kind of problem will, I believe, become ever more common in the future for a couple of reasons. First, with morality being increasingly relativized in society we will get more and more people coming to faith in Christ from a background where there is no recognition of right and wrong. These people will have repented because they will have recognised that they have sinned in some way. However, their concept of sin will be vague and there will be many things like cohabitation and homosexuality that they will not regard as sin because their culture does not.

Second, in our experience-orientated culture there will be more and more people who want to become Christians because they want the experience of being a Christian rather than because they want to repent and rid themselves of the guilt of sin. In other words, they are positively attracted to a relationship with a loving God rather than coming to that God in repentance because of fear of judgment. This will particularly be the case when they see how well their Christian friends have coped with crisis and heartbreak in their lives. They will find Christianity attractive because they find their Christian friends to be attractive people. This does not mean that repentance has never featured in their conversion, but that it has played a relatively minor part. People who become Christians in these circumstances will inevitably go through some kind of culture shock as they discover that they need to live a lifestyle that is holy.

The big question is how we deal with people who become Christians but have significant moral baggage. People are, of course, complex beings and therefore their lives will inevitably be complex. Anyone who suggests that these problems are easy to deal with or straightforward has never really been involved in pastoral work. Let me give a few examples to illustrate the kind of complexities involved.

After attending a series of family services, a family man called Gerald became a Christian. The church was delighted and immediately began a discipleship class with a view to baptising this new convert and bringing him into church membership. The family setting seemed ideal as Gerald gave the appearance of a happily married man with four lovely children. Gerald's wife showed little interest in becoming a Christian, but she was impressed with the changes that had taken place in her husband's life and thought that his going to church was a good thing. During one of the discipleship classes Gerald mentioned that he and his 'wife' had never actually been married. They had just cohabited for sixteen years and had never seen the need for marriage. It was put to Gerald that he really should be married before he could come into membership and, reluctantly, he agreed to talk to his partner about it. She reacted very badly, insisting that a legal document would not make their relationship any better, and stating that she felt insulted that he should try and revoke a decision they had made years ago just because the church was interfering.

In another case a self-employed businessman called Michael became a Christian through the witness of a Christian who was involved in the same industry. Again the setting seemed so ideal. This new Christian had a good job and a family and seemed to be a pillar of the community. It turned out, however, that Michael had been fiddling the books for many years, so as to avoid paying taxes. This kind of behaviour was so common and acceptable that he had never thought of it as being morally dubious. His whole lifestyle and the many bills which his lifestyle caused meant that tax evasion was virtually a necessity. Without it, he would have to make substantial reductions in his spending which in turn would cause great difficulties in his already struggling marriage.

A third case involved a woman in her mid-thirties who made a commitment to Christ. Jean had twice been married and divorced. One probable reason for the short-lived relationships was the residual effect of a difficult family background. Her father was physically and verbally abusive and that had left her badly scarred and emotionally damaged to the point where she struggled to trust men or have a stable relationship with them. Financially she was struggling, and this was made worse by the fact that she had two growing boys to look after. Jean had an affair with a married man who was much older than she. Her desperation for security and love drove her to continue this relationship even though she was not convinced that she loved the man. He was in the process of getting a divorce and, at the time of her conversion, they were making the final plans for their marriage.

The last example involves John, who is a single man in his early twenties. He is homosexual and has had a number of relationships in the past, though at the time of his conversion he was not involved with anyone. Because of the homophobic attitudes that John felt were rife in his area, he began to gravitate towards other homosexuals. He felt safer in bars and clubs where he would meet people with his own orientation. He obtained a mortgage that put him under considerable financial pressure and therefore wanted to find a lodger who would help to share the bills. He did not mind whether his lodger was male or female though, given his social life, the possibility of finding a lodger who was male and homosexual was really quite high. At that point John became a Christian and was introduced to the new world of the church that, he had always believed, was a thoroughly homophobic institution.

How should churches deal with such issues? How soon in our discipleship classes should we begin to deal with the moral baggage in people's lives? Should we require these new Christians to get their lives sorted out before they can become church members, and should they be able to participate in church services until this has happened?

Finding answers to these questions is notoriously difficult. By their very nature they are complex and the implications of any decision will necessarily be profound. There is no such thing as a simple solution when dealing with people's lives. Each church will also have particular practices which have a bearing. For example, in my church, it is possible to take the sacraments, that is be baptised and take communion, without actually becoming a member. In other churches, being baptised is tantamount to becoming a member and Christians cannot take part in communion without first being members of the church. Some churches even find themselves in the situation where a significant number of their members are not Christians anyway. Nevertheless, given that all of our churches will be different and have their own distinctives, there are some principles which we can identify that will help us in answering the basic question: what do we do with new Christians who carry a great deal of moral baggage with them?

Don't Run

The first thing we must do is ensure that we don't run away from any issue. Unfortunately many churches do just this. They do not want the hassle of trying to find answers to intractable problems and do not have the courage to grasp the nettle in dealing with people's lives. As a result, they tend to try and get rid of the problem altogether. This is done in a variety of ways ranging from telling the person directly that they are not welcome, to implying this by a generally unwelcoming attitude.

This, of course, is the easiest way to proceed. When churches do this they no longer have to face the problems that are caused by evangelism. It is neat and tidy, with no awkward customers to handle. But there are two fundamental problems with this approach. First, it is entirely unchristian for a church to behave in this way. Jesus had no hesitation helping people in need, even to the point where he was labelled a friend of sinners. Second, it is a very short-sighted policy. Given the moral decline in our society, it is unlikely that our evangelistic efforts will produce many converts with little or no moral baggage. Most people live lives that are a far cry from biblical standards because they live in a society that has altogether ignored what the Bible has to say. If churches insist on making it difficult for people like this to become part of the church, then the possibility of growth will greatly diminish. Consequently churches that are intolerant are churches that, in general, are dying out.

Biblical Standards

A second thing we must do in our churches is to maintain biblical standards. Although intolerance is not the answer, neither is compromise. The church in every age has to be aware of the danger of being assimilated into the world. Never is this danger more acute than when significant numbers of new converts bring with them their moral baggage. Indeed, one of the unfortunate consequences of many revivals is that the church has become increasingly immoral in their aftermath.

A balance needs to be maintained. The church needs to lovingly embrace new converts, with all their baggage, while at the same time communicating the clear message that we, as Christians, need to live God-honouring lives. If the standards which the church expects of its members begin to slip, that church will inevitably lose its cutting edge. This in turn will also lead to a slow death. A church with no standards will not be able to distinguish itself from the world around it. It will therefore not be in a position to call people out of the world. Having no standards, therefore, is just as unbiblical and short-sighted as intolerance towards new Christians with baggage.

A Christlike attitude

A third thing to keep in mind is the attitude of Jesus. During Christ's ministry he not only rubbed shoulders with people whose lives were in an intractable moral mess, he also dealt with their problems as they made their first few steps towards faith. As recorded in John 8 a woman was brought before Jesus having committed the act of adultery. The Pharisees who brought her asked Jesus for his opinion on whether or not she should be stoned to death for her crime, as demanded by the law of Moses.

Jesus brilliantly parried their attempt to trap him and then focused his attention on the woman herself. His words to her were beautiful and strong. He first told her that he did not condemn her, even though he knew of her guilt. This brings to mind Jesus' statement that he came not to condemn but to save, (John 3:17; 12:47.)[1]. Having said that, Jesus went on to insist that this woman's proper response to mercy should be to stop sinning. Here we have a picture of Christ forgiving and refusing to condemn, but balancing this with the insistence that a holy life is a must. This balance is not easy to maintain, but the church needs to learn to imitate Christ.

Remember They Are 'Babies'

A fourth thing that we need to bear in mind is that new Christians are spiritual babies (1 Pet.2:2). It would be entirely unreasonable to expect a baby to drive a car, hold down a secure job or work out your income tax. This kind of activity can only be done with a measure of maturity. Babies and children also have to be taught what is right and wrong as their sense of values is in need of fine tuning. Parents therefore do not let their children make big decisions for themselves until they are capable of doing so.

In much the same way, the Bible pictures new Christians as spiritual babies. They are not in a position to make mature and informed decisions about their lifestyles. They obviously want to follow Christ, and have repented, but that does not mean that they understand what is appropriate or inappropriate behaviour for a Christian. They will also be inclined to make mistakes and fall, just as normal babies do. In addition, adults who

1   Carson, *The Gospel According to John*, p.337

become Christians do not begin their Christian lives within a vacuum. Rather, their starting point is at a time when bad habits have already been formed and attitudes about what is right and wrong are calcified.

We should not be surprised, then, if new Christians struggle to lead holy lives and find it very difficult to break the sinful habit patterns of the past. The church should not condemn them, but should care for them as parents and re-educate them so that they can begin to live holy lives. This may take some time! Spiritual maturity and the discernment that it brings does not come about overnight. I have worked with Christians who have been struggling with big moral issues in their lives for years after their conversion. While not compromising on the standards that it expects, the church needs to demonstrate patience and not develop the attitude that new Christians should be pounced upon as soon as they make a mistake. If a new convert does get drunk, stumbles sexually or behaves unwisely, it does not invalidate his claim to be a follower of Christ. Rather, it means that, as a spiritual baby, he is struggling to come to terms with his new found faith. These issues need to be handled lovingly and sensitively.

The Wider Picture

Fifth, each person within the church is an individual, and each case needs to be taken on its own merits. As a church we need to be aware, when we are dealing with young Christians and their problems, which wider issues may be involved and other people need to be taken into consideration. Take the case of Gerald as an example. Although he was living with a woman to whom he was not married, and had children by her, his wife was not a Christian and therefore could not be expected to have a biblical view of marriage. Certainly the church leaders would be wise to explain to Gerald's wife why the church values marriage so much. However, they would have no authority to demand that she agree to marriage, neither should Gerald be coerced into putting her under any pressure as this could jeopardise their relationship. In such a situation there is no right answer, but there are wrong ones. In my judgment, it would be wrong to deny Gerald membership of the church even though his relationship is clearly wrong. He was in a situation that had wider ramifications and these needed to be taken into consideration.

Acute and Chronic Problems

A final thing that we need to consider is whether or not this issue is something that is an ongoing habit pattern or is it is just a mistake that the new Christian has made. In one sense it should make no difference because sin is sin. On the other hand, a person's intention needs to be taken into account.

Take the issue of drunkenness for example. In our society the excessive consumption of alcohol is hardly unknown. Indeed for many, the weekend is reserved for drinking sprees and hang-overs. There is a difference between someone who regularly gets drunk, and has the intention of doing so, and someone who has an occasional drink and perhaps consumes a little too much. In both cases there is a degree of intoxication, but one is certainly more serious than the other and, pastorally, must be treated as such. I know a number of young Christians who come from homes where alcohol is available in abundance and where family members are often drunk. If a young Christian in such circumstances were to get drunk regularly it would be a cause of great concern, and the church would certainly have to exercise discipline. However, if that same person occasionally made a mistake and took too much, given the whole culture of drinking from which they came I think a little understanding would be more appropriate that the heavy hand of discipline. I am not saying that getting drunk is acceptable for a Christian, nor am I saying that this should not receive pastoral attention. But I am differentiating between a chronic problem and one which is no more than a regrettable incident.

These guidelines do not in themselves answer the question of how we deal with new Christians who bring with them a great deal of moral baggage. These issues are still very difficult to deal with and often our response should be one of damage limitation as no perfect solution exists. However, if applied, these guidelines will help a church to move forward, taking each case on its own merits, and cutting a path along which the church and the new Christian can proceed to their mutual benefit.

One crucial element that must not be lost sight of is the necessity of these new Christians growing in their faith. These issues are best worked out if the new Christian begins to develop spiritual maturity. The key to seeing this growth, and a biblical lifestyle emerging as a result, is for more mature Christians to role model the Christian life and mentor their young brothers and sisters in Christ. There is no substitute for a Christian friend who is close enough to the person to see what is needed, and encouraging enough to enable the person to take steps towards spiritual maturity.

Emotional Baggage

Another type of baggage is the emotional sort. This, too, is on the increase. I have long been of the opinion that most people, emotionally speaking, are held together by scar tissue. Life takes its toll on people in the modern world. Work pressures, family crises, marital breakdown, abuse and bereavement have left many people wounded and hurting. A significant proportion of people who become Christians will carry some of these hurts with them into their new found faith. Indeed throughout history the church has often been perceived by society as a caring place, a sanctuary where life's victims can find comfort and acceptance. This is good because it demonstrates that the church has fulfilled its role of caring for those for whom no one else cares. But the result of this has been that the church has often attracted people who are damaged emotionally.

The pastoral burden that many churches have to carry is both enormous and growing. In our postmodern age people are very absorbed with their own needs and have a great desire to share these needs with others. This desire for 'opening up' and sharing feelings is so strong that the talk shows have turned people's problems into a voyeuristic art form. Discussing your problems with individuals or an audience is the therapy of this new millennium. Anyone who is involved in church leadership will confirm that increasing numbers of people in our churches want to bring their burdens to the leadership of the church in the hope of finding help. No longer do people put up with it and keep a stiff upper lip. Rarely do we meet people who want to suffer in silence. The openness of our culture has brought everyone's skeletons out of the cupboard and into public gaze.

In much the same way as some churches struggle to deal with all the moral baggage that comes their way, they also stagger under the weight of all the emotional baggage. This baggage is often roughly treated by Christian leaders intolerant of the needs of those to whom they minister. I have heard horror stories of wounded people who have sought help from the leaders of their church only to be told to 'get a grip' of themselves and stop attention-seeking. In some cases this response comes from leaders who feel overwhelmed by the great need and their increasing pastoral responsibilities. Sadly, in other cases it is simply because leaders can sometimes be impatient and lacking in genuine compassion.

How do we begin to deal with the enormous pastoral issues that arise? This is a huge issue because if we do not lovingly care for the new converts that come to our churches for sanctuary, they will leave concluding that the church is not a place for them after all. Once bitten they will be unlikely ever to return to church as they have received the message that church only accepts people who come with no baggage or problems. So how do we deal with these emotional problems?

Don't Duck Any Problems

The first thing we must do, as we care for emotionally damaged people, is ensure that we ignore no one. In much the same way as we avoid people who carry moral baggage with them, it is easy to avoid people with emotional problems. This should never be the case. In some cases, people present problems that to the casual observer seem trite and insignificant. To the person to whom it is a problem, however, it may well be a big issue. It should therefore not be treated as something trivial. Other problems are much more serious and demand a great deal of thought and attention. This must be given, recognising that everyone is precious in God's sight and is loved by him. In short no one should be ignored.

Be Prepared for the Long Haul

A second thing that needs to be borne in mind is that people are not machines that can be fixed quickly. My car, though old, is able to function well with the occasional oil change and a bit of servicing. If anything goes wrong, my friends at the local garage can have it fixed in a matter of hours. Not so with people. We are highly complex beings and our emotional makeup is full of complexity. Some people have the capacity to bounce back after problems and keep going, others simply cannot. Some of the people who come to our churches will be carrying emotional scars that run deep and have been causing pain for years. It is entirely unrealistic to imagine that these issues will disappear

after a few weeks of loving church fellowship. Certainly the
warmth of church life is of great help to people who are struggling, but the scars can take years to heal. The work of pastoral
care is very long-term indeed and will require considerable
patience and perseverance.

Treat Every Person with Sensitivity

It goes without saying that the wounded people who come to us
need to be treated with sensitivity. They are already suffering
and do not need curt remarks or an attitude that says, 'You are
a burden to me.' Some of us find it difficult to be sensitive, but
it is an attitude of heart that must be cultivated. Without sensitivity, the emotional baggage that our church members carry
will get more acute rather than lessen. Churches should be
havens where emotionally damaged people feel safe and have
the confidence to deal with the issues that haunt them.

Look to God for Healing

It is also vital that we recognise God's role in our pastoral care.
The people to whom we minister were created by God in the
first place, so he knows better than we what they need. In his
omniscience, God knows exactly what circumstances have
caused the damage and, surely, the remedy that will bring healing. I have often found myself in a situation where I really don't
know what to do for the person I am trying to help, or even
what to say to them. Human fallibility greatly limits our pastoral effectiveness. In such circumstances prayer and listening to
God is the only way forward. But when we do this we must
believe that God can and will make a difference, and will bring
healing to the wounded person that we are caring for. Faith is
therefore a vital component in pastoral work.

Beware of being Swallowed by the Monster of Dependence

From a practical point of view it is important to bear in mind
that, although the church needs to care for people who are hurting, wisdom is also needed in deciding just what level of help to
give and how it should be given. There are two potential problems that can result from handling emotional baggage. First, it
is possible for church leaders to become so wrapped up in people's problems that they neglect their other duties. This can be a
very real problem because some people would absorb all of a

leader's available time and still ask for more. Second, a person with emotional baggage could become so wrapped up in themselves that they begin to find security in their problems and do not want to move on and deal with them. What is more, their self-absorption will prevent them from being able to make any kind of contribution to the wider life of the church. Their problems must therefore be dealt with.

This does not mean that we should pull back on our compassion for hurting people. That should never be the case. But we do need to exercise wisdom, otherwise everyone ends up losing in the long run. In my church, we have tried to come up with a policy on pastoral care. We are willing to help anyone and spend as much time with them as is needed, provided they are willing to do something about their problems. While fully recognising that these could be long-term, we expect to see a measure of progress. In addition, we want to see at least a desire on the part of the people we are helping to be part of the church and to make a contribution. This contribution may well be small, but we want to see people giving and not just taking all the time. If these conditions are met, then we are more than happy to invest in their troubled lives. If not, then we will not commit very much time and energy to them. This may sound harsh, but it is a realistic necessity.

Questions

1 To what extent does your church successfully handle the baggage that new Christians bring with them?
2 What obstacles might prevent your church from handling these situations well, and what should be done about it?
3 How does a church get the balance between being tolerant and being holy?
4 How would you go about educating your church as to how to handle baggage?

13

To Do or Die
(Reach the World)

As I travel around the country one of the most shocking sights that I come across is that of church buildings that are abandoned, turned into bingo halls or trendy flats, or just used as dumping grounds for the local community. It is a shock not only because church buildings should never be used in this way, but because so many in this country are no longer being used for the purpose of worship.

Crises of this magnitude do not resolve themselves. There needs to be some intervention if this haemorrhaging is to be stopped. In 1914 Lord Kitchener was appointed as war minister to lead the battle against the Germans. His motto was a simple 'Britain needs you' and no one of that generation could have escaped the stern and challenging look of Kitchener's face and pointed finger on the thousands of posters dotted all over the country. But his call to mobilisation worked and some 3,000,000 joined the armed services.

The church today needs a similar clarion call. We are in the midst of the greatest battle of human history, one that has been waged continually in every corner of the earth since the fall. It is the battle for men's souls. God in his great mercy has brought about revivals all over the world and revival is well overdue in the United Kingdom today. Though revival is the sovereign work of God, as his church we still have the obligation to reach out to a dying world with the message of hope and life through the death of Christ. This message is our world's only hope.

As I have tried to point out in this book, the problem is that the church is all too often out of touch and remote from the community to which it is sent with the gospel. This must change if there is to be any hope for our friends, colleagues and neighbours who do not know Jesus Christ for themselves. We must act now!

Action, however, will only come about if Christians want to be busy in the work of evangelism. Sadly, my experience has been that many Christians are simply not motivated enough when it comes to the difficult business of sharing the gospel with others. All too many Christians let an opportunity pass, rather than speak up and say something that will make friends and colleagues think about their spiritual needs. Few take the trouble to create opportunities in which they will be able to say something. If this situation persists, then the days ahead will be dark for many churches in the United Kingdom. The situation is urgent and we must act now.

Questions

1 What barriers are preventing your church from being an effective centre of evangelism and what should be done about this?
2 What steps will you personally take to ensure that you are an effective witness for Jesus Christ?

For Further Reading

Useful Books on Apologetics

Apologetics: An Introduction by William Lane Craig (Moody)
   This is the best introduction I have read on the subject of apologetics. It is well laid out and uses compelling arguments.

Can Man Live without God? by Ravi Zacharias (Word)
   This is a well written and powerfully argued apologetic showing why society needs to believe in God.

Darwin on Trial by Philip Johnson (Monarch)
   Johnson uses his sharp lawyer's mind to attack the logic of Darwinism.

Know Why you Believe by Paul Little (IVP)
   This is a brief but helpful guide to apologetics and covers many issues in a limited amount of space. Excellent if you have not read books before on apologetics.

No Easy Answers by William Lane Craig (Moody)
   This short book looks at the problems of suffering, doubt and unanswered prayer and gives an appropriate Christian response.

Scaling the Secular City by J.P. Moreland (Baker)
   Moreland tackles secularism head on and defends Christianity against science, as well as demonstrating its intellectual coherence.

Useful Books on Culture and Postmodernity

A Primer on Postmodernism by Stanley Grenz (Eerdmans)
   This is an excellent introduction to postmodernism.

Evangelicals and Truth by Peter Hicks (IVP)
   This book looks at how postmodernity affects our concept of truth, and defends the Christian belief in God as the basis of our concept of truth.

The Gagging of God by Don Carson (Zondervan)
   This substantial work deals in great detail with pluralism influenced by these notions which is a symptom of postmodernity. Carson gives some useful ideas on evangelism in a society.

Truth Decay by Douglas Groothuis (IVP)
   This is a very helpful introduction to postmodernism, and it demonstrates how truth is eroded to the detriment of society.

Bibliography

BEBBINGTON, D.W., *Evangelicalism in Modern Britain*, Routledge, 1989

BRIERLEY, Peter, UK Christian Handbook 2000/2001, *Religious Trends*, No.2, HarperCollins

BROWN, Colin, *Christianity & Western Thought* Vol.1, Apollos, 1990

BRUCE, F.F., *The Book of Acts*, New London Commentary, Marshall Morgan & Scott, 1968

CANE, Herbert, *The Christian World Mission: Today and Tomorrow*, Baker, 1981

CARSON, Don, *The Gagging of God*, Zondervan, 1996

CARSON, Don, *The Gospel According to John*, IVP, 1991

CHEESMAN, Graham, *Hyperchoice*, IVP, 1998

COLLINSON, Diane, *Fifty Major Philosophers*, Routledge, 1997

COPLEY, Terence, *About the Bible*, Bible Society, 1990

CRAIGIE, Peter, *Psalms 1-50*, WBC vol.19, Word, 1986

CRAIG, William L, *Apologetics: An Introduction*, Moody Press, 1984

DEMBSKI, William Ed., *Mere Creation*, IVP, 1998

DRANE, John, *Cultural Change and Biblical Faith*, Paternoster, 2000

EDEN, Martyn Ed., *Britain on the Brink*, Crossway Books, 1990

ERICKSON, Millard, *Christian Theology*, Baker Books, 1998

GAY, Craig, *The Way of the Modern World*, Eerdmans/Paternoster, 1998

GILL, David, *The Book of Acts in its First Century Setting*, Vol.2, Ed. D. Gill & C. Gempf, Eerdmans/Paternoster, 1994

GRENZ, Stanley, *A Primer on Postmodernism*, Eerdmans, 1996

GROOTHUIS, Douglas, *Truth Decay*, IVP, 2000

HALL, D.R., *Illustrated Bible Dictionary*, IVP, 1980

JOHNSTONE, Patrick, *Operation World*, (6th edition) Paternoster Lifestyle, 2001

JOHNSTON, Phillip, *Darwin on Trial*, Monarch, 1991

JOSEPHUS, *The Complete Works of Josephus*, Kregel, 1981

KORAN, *The Koran*, Penguin Books, 1990 edition

LARKIN, William, *Acts*, New Testament Commentary, IVP, 1995

LEUPOLD, H.C., *Exposition of Psalms*, Baker, 1990

LEWIS, C.S., *God in the Dock*, Collins, 1979

LITTLE, Paul, *Know Why You Believe*, IVP, 2000

LONGENECKER, Richard, *Acts*, Expositor's Bible Commentary, Zondervan, 1995

MARCH, Ruth, *Europe Reborn*, OM Publishing, 1992

MARSHALL, I. Howard, *Acts*, TNTC, IVP, 1980

MCDOWELL, Josh, *The Resurrection Factor*, Here's Life Publishers, 1981

MCQUOID, Stephen, *A Guide to God's Family*, Partnership, 2000

MCQUOID, Stephen, *A New Kind of Living*, Christian Focus Publications, 1998

MICHAELS, Ramsey, *1 Peter*, Word Biblical Commentary, Word, 1988

MOO, Douglas, *The Epistle to the Romans*, Eerdmans, 1996

MURRAY, Stuart, *Church Planting*, Paternoster Press, 1998

NORTON, Mark, Texts and Manuscripts of the Old Testament, Ed. P.W. Comfort, *The Origin of the Bible*, Tyndale, 1992

PALEY, William, *Natural Theology*, Ed. John Hick, 'The Existence of God', Macmillan, 1964

SMITH, Linda, *A Brief Guide to Ideas*, Lion, 1997

RUSSELL, Bertrand, *History of Western Philosophy*, Routledge, 1991

SINE, Tom, *Mustard Seed versus McWorld*, Monarch, 1999

STOLL, David, *Is Latin America Turning Protestant?*, University of California Press, 1990

STOTT, John, *The Message of Acts*, BST, IVP, 1990

TOFFLER, Alvin, *Future Shock*, Pan Books, 1973

VEITH, Gene, *Guide to Contemporary Culture*, Crossway Books, 1994

WANAMAKER, Charles, *The Epistle to the Thessalonians*, Commentary on the Greek Text, Eerdmans/Paternoster, 1990

WILLIAMS, Peter, *The Case for God*, Monarch, 1999

ZACHARIAS, Ravi, *Jesus among other Gods*, Word Books, 2000

ZACHARIAS, Ravi, *Can Man Live without God?*, Word Books, 1994